ALSO BY THE FIRESIGN THEATRE

The Complete Plays of The Firesign Theatre

"Anythynge You Want To"
"Marching To Shibboleth"
"Exorcism In Your Daily Life"

By Taylor Jessen and The Firesign Theatre
"Duke of Madness Motors"
The Complete "Dear Friends" Radio Era
"Box of Danger"
The Complete Nick Danger Casebook

By Peter Bergman
with David Ossman and Phil Fountain
"Trolling The Woe"

By David Ossman
"Dr. Firesign's Follies"
"The Ronald Reagan Murder Case"

The Firesign Theatre
firesigntheatre.com

PROFILES IN BARBEQUE SAUCE

**The Psychedelic Firesign Theatre
On Stage — 1967-1972**

The Complete Plays of
The Firesign Theatre
Volume 4
4 or 5 Crazee Books
2012

PROFILES IN BARBEQUE SAUCE
The Psychedelic Firesign Theatre
On Stage — 1967–1972
Copyright (c) 2012

BY PHILIP AUSTIN, PETER BERGMAN, DAVID OSSMAN AND PHILIP PROCTOR

ALL RIGHTS RESERVED.

No part of this book may be reproduced in any form or by any means, electronic, mechanical, digital, photocopying, or recording, except for in the inclusion of a review, without permission in writing from the publisher.

Published in the USA by:
BEARMANOR MEDIA
P.O. BOX 71426
ALBANY, GEORGIA 31708
www.BearManorMedia.com

"Thanksgiving" and "A Shadow Moves Upon A Land" © 2012 by Phil Austin

Photo and Re-print Credits:
Most Photographs by John Rose.
John Carpenter's interview published in the Los Angeles Free Press, Oct 10, 1969.
Love-In poster by Gary Grimshaw, 1967.
Love-In story from the Los Angeles Herald-Examiner, March 27, 1967.
Santa Monica Civic Benefit poster by Genie Riley.
Bergman on the Hopi from the Los Angeles Oracle, Vol. 1, No. 1, March 1967.
"Temporarily Humboldt County — An American Pageant" published by Broadway Play Publishing, 2012.
Hopi Elder's photo by Marv Lyons, March 1967.
"Theater" column by Mark Shipper published in Open City, issue of March 22-28, 1968.
Ice House reviews appeared in Variety (2/15/68)
and the L.A. Times (2/21/68)
Mixville Rocket (1970-1971) edited by David Ossman.
Rocket logo by Tinika.
Comic page by Phil Austin.
Selections from "Firesign: An Interview," published in Touch, 6/6/73.

Rights to perform these Firesign Theatre radio and stage plays are available from the Authors. Please query Comedic Rights at www.firesigntheatre.com. Rights to perform "Waiting For The Electrician," "Nick Danger," "Don't Crush That Dwarf" and "Temporarily Humboldt County" in versions adapted for the stage are available from www.broadwayplaypubl.com.

The Firesign Theatre's website is **firesigntheatre.com**

ISBN-10: 1-59393-551-X (alk. paper)
ISBN-13: 978-1-59393-551-1 (alk. paper)

Printed in the United States of America.

Edited by David Ossman
Cover design by Phil Fountain, Oz Design Group.
Designed by Valerie Thompson.

First Edition.

Our Founder

Contents

PROFILES IN BARBEQUE SAUCE
The Psychedelic Firesign Theatre On Stage — 1967-1972

FIRST HITS

International Youth On Parade 9

Temporarily Humboldt County . . . 19

W. C. Fields Forever . . . 30

38 Cunegonde . . . 37

A Shadow Moves Upon A Land . . . 45

Freek for a Week . . . 65

Profiles in Barbeque Sauce . . . 83

TOKES AT THE 'GROVE

Thanksgiving, or Pass The Indian Please! . . . 98

The Fuse of Doom . . . 107

The Count of Monte Cristo . . . 127

. . . nd Of The World . . . 136

The TV Set . . . 143

Mutt 'n' Smutt . . . 175

The Dr. Blojob Show . . . 186

The Ash Grove Encore . . . 194

The Bob Sideburn News . . . 204

SPACED OUT

The Martian Space Party . . . 217

DR. FIRESIGN'S TRAVELING ANTIQUE CIRCUS

by John Carpenter
Los Angeles Free Press, Oct. 10, 1969

Three years ago Peter Bergman was doing the first of the many manifestations of Radio Free Oz on KPFK. Phil Proctor was in town working for the East Village Other and appearing in a play. David Ossman was an executive with the ABC network, hanging about KPFK doing a documentary on the American Indian. And Phil Austin was director of literature and drama for the station. Bergman's program was, at the time, almost a religious cult to many listeners who would phone in to have their Tarot read by Peter the Wizard, or hear the collages he prepared.

Starting with the Oz Film Festival, where The Nun and other dirty pictures were shown on the radio for the first time, the four got together frequently to do satire and perform radio skits. After a few months the show moved from KPFK where it had been on five nights a week over to KRLA where it was on every Sunday night for almost a year.

The group was signed by Columbia Records to do an album, "Waiting for the Electrician or Someone Like Him," and started appearing weekly at the Magic Mushroom doing live radio dramas from the club's stage that were also broadcast over KRLA. One night Bergman read a commercial over the air, "Put you hands up the skirt of a Toyota and really turn on," and after a short period off the air, turned up on KMET Sunday mornings solo doing a DJ and talk show.

The show, "Son of Radio Free Oz," was cancelled after Bergman played the Fugs' "Johnny Pissoff Meets the Red Angel."

The following interview was taped in the Board Room of Columbia Records.

CARPENTER: How did the Firesign Theatre start?

BERGMAN: Proctor and I had a blind date when I was at Yale and . . .

PROCTOR: No, we had a good feeling between us, so to speak. Then we started doing this radio program which I call Bregman.

BERGMAN: It's Bergman.

PROCTOR: Birdman, that's right. He was known at the time as the Birdman of KPFK because they kept him in this little office, a closet it was — with bars though. The show was called Radio Free Ooze. Later it was changed to the Electric Brew, due to the influence of out first record. My first lover, Phil, was working as a program manager at KPFK, and my second lover, Davey or Davey Beck to his friends . . .

BERGMAN: Like Olga?

PROCTOR: . . . was working as an announcer and best boy at the station, so the four of us, counting Peter, did a put-on, a hoax. The first hoax was the Oz Film Festival. We showed a dirty movie on the radio, yes, which got us into a lot of trouble. After that, we did a lot of skits on the radio all of which were a lot of bunk. I was writing articles and doing collages for the East Village Other at the time, and I knew Peter from Yale.

I was with Peter Fonda and Brandon De Wilde and we were at the Sunset Strip riot doing research for a movie about the Youth Revolution called "Easy Rider" . . . It has changed a great deal since then . . . Well, at the Sunset Strip riot, I sat on a picture of Bergren when the police pushed us into this Happy Pup, a homosexual restaurant. I looked at it and it said, "KPFK newsman," and I said, "Gee, I know him. Maybe he can get me a place to sleep." I spent the next three weeks in the KPFK studio curled up under a big table while Peter was rapping on the radio.

OSSMAN: I was an ABC executive then. I was down at KPFK trying to convince Peter Indians would be interesting. I knocked on the closet door and this muffled voice came out from inside, "Peter! What about doing something on the Indians?" "On what? What about Indians?"

PROCTOR: I went on tour in a play with Robert Cummings. We played nine months (or was it six weeks?) in Florida.

	Then I went to New York and spent some time with Diana Dew who was making electric dresses at the time.
BERGMAN:	Were you [illegible] her?
PROCTOR:	I was back in New York at the end of a rope, and I got this call from Bergman. "The Firesign Theatre is making a record." "The who?" "The Firesign Theatre. I thought it would be a good name for our group." "What group?" "The guys we did the skits with on radio; it's all set. Columbia Records is picking up your ticket." After that I packed up my apartment and walked across country speaking only Russian 'cause I wanted to do what my great great grandfather had done.
CARPENTER:	What was that?
PROCTOR:	He was tried as a Communist before it was in vogue.
BERGMAN:	Yes. That was in Vogue just last week.
PROCTOR:	I walked into Peter's house and he said, "Speak English. You can sleep in the attic with the dogs and ants. We start recording next week." I said fine, and moved in three weeks later. We were in the studio a lot.
CARPENTER:	You had all worked in radio individually?
AUSTIN:	In high school I did a thing called the Tension Convention by the Four Candidates. That was my first group. Me and this friend of mine did collages then. Now I'm doing the same thing and making a living at it.
BERGMAN:	The first of the three times I've been kicked off the air was at Shaker Heights High School. I did a Chinese takeover on the school station that linked together all the rooms of the school. I go on one morning and I did the national anthem, then went right into a Chinese opera and said "Good morning" in this horrible Chinese accent.

PROCTOR: I was schooled entirely in the East. I was in a gang — Dayton Dallas and Quen Robinson. Dayton Dallas is now a hot rod motorcycle rider and Quen has fallen off a garage.

CARPENTER: How did "Waiting for the Electrician" do?

BERGMAN: It's doing really well now, but it started slow. I remember when it first came out we got this call from this guy and he says, "You're dead in New York. It stinks. Clive Davis, president of Columbia Records, thinks it's in bad taste. You're dead in New York," and we said a lot of things are dead in New York. The company dropped us. Then when the record started getting played and started selling, John McClure went into some executive meeting with it and waved it around saying, "You guys don't know what's going on. Leave them alone. Let them do their thing, but don't fire them." It worked, so we got to go in and did the second album.

PROCTOR: It was just, "You're dead in New York; that's it; over," but we just kept on doing what we always did. We did live shows at the Magic Mushroom, benefits, and played the Ash Grove the weekend Bobby Kennedy was killed, and also were there the night Martin Luther King got it. It was weird, all those people there to be made to laugh, the hardest audience in the world . . .

BERGMAN: Remember what happened? Nobody laughed at all. We did "Profiles in Barbecue Sauce," remember?

AUSTIN: See, now we were playing outside of the Mushroom. We had a club act, costumes, we had a manager, all of these things came together at the same time, at one common point. So we said, "Well, we're a theatrical troupe. We will do theatre." We even had a set, and we said, "Get your shabby little set, and get your moth-eaten costumes and put on something fantastic for the people." That was our image of ourselves, and it worked.

CARPENTER: I used to hear a lot of talk about doing street theater, gypsy-like all over LA; are you still into that?

AUSTIN: That was Peter's trip, we were going to go around to all the communes at one time, but . . . you know . . . where are they?

OSSMAN: We came out with the props and the full theatre.

PROCTOR: I went to see the Congress of Wonders, and I thought they were into the same trip we are, you know; we'd never known there was anyone like us. They did it the logical way and played to the Fillmore audience, and we were out in left field somewhere.

BERGMAN: Comic strips — that is what we were doing. We didn't know what it was.

OSSMAN: It was a put-on theater, in the tradition of the old touring shows, "Dr. Firesign's Antique Traveling Circus."

CARPENTER: When did the car dealer, Ralph Spoilsport come into your act?

OSSMAN: Peter had taken some gorgeous woman off to Europe to make a movie . . .

BERGMAN: Turkey, yes.

OSSMAN: Proctor and his old lady and me and my old lady were living in this big hilltop house while he was over there, and one day Phil walked down the stairs and did it. He said, "I have just worked out the Ralph Williams Mantra." "Huh," we said, and then he did it and we were on the floor.

PROCTOR: Hiya, friends . . .

OSSMAN: When Peter came back I said, "Phil's got the perfect Ralph Williams Mantra, you know, and he spends a good deal of time in the bathroom because of it." Ralph became Ralph Spoilsport, one of the sponsors of "Freek for a Week," one of our radio skits. He was great, always a guaranteed laugh and gradually all of us began to be able to do that voice.

PROCTOR: We had discovered the American salesman. Two things happened to Ralph after that. He got written into the "How Can You Be In Two Places At Once, When You're Not Anywhere At All" side of the record, which was to be his apotheosis. The apotheosis of Ralph Williams because he talks over himself five times. All of us do it. Peter picked it up and started using it on the Jack Poet ads — it's identified with those as well.

OSSMAN: Here we were, sitting on this record and all of a sudden everyone is doing Ralph. He goes on . . .

PROCTOR: Carson! Instead of feeling sorry for ourselves, we realized we had predicted the appearance of Williams on the Carson show doing a take-off on himself. We did it first. We predicted it.

CARPENTER: I read about a put-on you did at the Columbia Convention.

PROCTOR: Yes, all of the Columbia people from all over the world were there and we did a put-on. I got up at the podium and we had slides and tapes. I introduced myself as Peter Savatte, who represented EuroPulse. Peter was in Europe acting in a movie and sent us a tape from Paris. He was Paul Alcorn and David was Professor Lowenthal.

I said, "At EuroPulse we have determined that the buying public is the youth market. What are the youth? In order to determine this, we at EuroPulse have determined that we had to do what youth do. We smoked pot, we sniffed glue, we dropped acid — some of us found the tabs and took them. But, so that we wouldn't lose touch with reality, we drank too. Heavily."

Dr. Firesign's Traveling Antique Circus: by John Carpenter

FROM EAST TO WEST IT WAS "IN" DAY
6000 Hippies Stage 'Love-In' at Elysian Park

Los Angeles Herald-Examiner, Monday, March 27, 1967
by Gene Youngblood and Cliff Blackburn

A pungent odor of incense lingered in the thickets of Elysian Park today after Los Angeles' first major "Love-In" — a fanciful celebration which attracted some 6000 hippies and onlookers Easter Sunday.

The Love-In also attracted hate.

At least three persons attending the fairy tale festivity were seriously beaten by gangs of neighborhood youths who staged several rock, bottle and club-flailing attacks on pedestrians who thronged the area from 6 a.m. until 10 p.m.

One victim, Thompson Thayer Guild, 18, a student of Pacific Palisades, was set upon by a gang of children 10 to 12 years old and was reported in critical condition at General Hospital where physicians said he may lose his right eye.

Traffic in and out of the area was heavily congested most of the day. Hundreds of celebrants, dressed outlandishly in period costumes, "freak" clothes and Bohemian attire, walked as far as two miles from their cars to the scene.

In the park itself, sound was the overwhelming sensation. Nearly everyone, it seemed, carried flutes and shook tambourines and bells. Three rock and roll bands, their driving sounds supercharged by enormous amplifiers, added to the spirit of the day.

Men wore East Indian saris or American Indian blankets and braided their long hair. Girls wore mini-skirts and painted their legs psychedelic colors. Picnickers passed out their food free to passersby. Children and oldsters danced on the grass like Pans in a rite of spring.

INTERNATIONAL YOUTH ON PARADE

Performed on Radio Free Oz, KPFK-FM
February 15, 1967

ORIGINAL CAST
Philip Austin — Michelle

Peter Bergman — Host

David Ossman — Voices

Philip Proctor — Jean Turmoile

INTERNATIONAL YOUTH ON PARADE

PETER: The Oz Firesign Theatre, in cooperation with —

PHIL P: The Belgian Radio and Television Service

PETER: Das Deutsche Rund und Blaupunkt Gesellschaft

DAVID: The All-India Radio Pakistan Blue Network

PHIL P: El Radio Servicio Internacional Bolivia

PHIL A: The BBC Home Service

DAVID: ...and the BBC Tea Service

PHIL P: Ici Paris, Radio Diffusion Francaise

PHIL P: All People Radio Free People's Republic, Peking Radio

PHIL A: And outasite radio in Boss Angeles, KPFK!

PETER: Presents — INTERNATIONAL YOUTH ON PARADE.

ALL "SING" ("Dum-dum-dee-dum"): "STOUTHEARTED MEN" — CONTINUE UNDER

PETER: The world today is in a peck of trouble. Disrespect and turmoil are everywhere. From Maine to California, across the wide blue oceans, on continents all over the wide world, in far and widely distant lands — wherever the sun shines, there is disrespect and turmoil. And everywhere where there is disrespect and turmoil, there is youth. International youth on parade!

SINGING UP, THEN OUT

PETER: Well, folks, here we are in Paris. Land of the Eiffel Tower.

ALL SING: MAIN THEME TO "AMERICAN IN PARIS"

SOUND: GENERAL HUBUB & TRAFFIC

PETER: A significant group of French students have gathered here under the beautiful Arc de Triomphe to protest the state of international youth. And I have with me the spokesman of the group . . .

JEAN: I am Jean Turmoil, and I'm very happy to be able to talk to the world in this way. (OFF) Ah, je ne sais pas!

PETER: Jean, could you tell the audience — what is the nature of your protest today?

JEAN: Well, for the first time, we are trying a technique borrowed from the American friends. It is the Love-In. There is not enough love in the world. There is not enough love between different political factions. There is not enough love between forces of the Communist and the Fascist in our society. There is not enough love between the older people, the younger people — there is not enough love between me and anybody! This is the only time I get to love anybody!

PETER: Well, what is different about the method and technique? I notice there's a very interesting scene going on here under the picturesque Arc de Triomphe.

JEAN: Yes, you notice, this for the first time is not only the male students who are going to be beaten up. We have today both the coeducational and the female students. And you will notice that...

MICHELLE: Ah ma petit fromage, Jean... (KISSES HIM)

JEAN: Oh, excuse me a moment... Michelle! Comment ca va... Michelle, look, je pas surreal et maintenaint I can't talk to you. Go lie down... Ah yes, I'm sorry.

PETER: You were saying that this Love-In is different from your other protests. How is that?

JEAN: Well, I would like to explain first of all that the gendarmes usually attack us with leaden cloak, you know? So for the first time we have put in leaden blankets and stop the traffic pattern, you see? We have led them out here, and every...

MICHELLE: Mon petit plum, Jean! (KISSES HIM)

JEAN: I'm sorry... Michelle! (MUTTERS IN FRENCH – AD LIB)

PETER: I think the audience is... Jean? Jean, I think the audience is really interested in knowing, what is the political manifestation of this protest?

JEAN: Yes, well, first of all I want to make very clear: We are not le Communiste. We are not Fascist...

MICHELLE: Petit Jean... (KISSES HIM) (AD LIB)

JEAN: Michelle: Je ne pas pas!

PETER: Where do you think...excuse me Jean, if I could just have a few minutes of your time. Just where do you think the protest here is going to go in terms of international youth?

JEAN: We want to go all the way to the top. We are going to the minister...

MICHELLE: Jean! (MUTTERS IN FRENCH – AD LIB)

JEAN: Michelle, please... Ah, oui? Maintenaint? It's beginning?

PETER: Well, that's very interesting — you say the Minister...?

JEAN: Oui, oui, but it's starting! It's starting! I've got to get over there with Michelle right now. À bientôt, babes!... Michelle! Attend!

ALL SING:	LA MARSEILLAISE (CONTINUES UNDER) Allons enfants de la Patrie, Le jour de gloire est arrive... (Vive la liberté!)
PETER:	And as the sun sets over the picturesque writhing bodies under the picturesque Arc de Triomphe, we bid a picturesque farewell to Paris . . .
JEAN:	Ah, Michelle...
PETER:	. . . Historical land of love and lovers.
JEAN:	Michelle! Ma belle!
RECORD:	BEATLES "MICHELLE" PLAYS OUT

PETER BERGMAN ON THE HOPI INDIAN

Excerpts from an extended Wizardly Rap with Tom Schulz, Editor, Oracle, City of Los Angeles, Vol. 1, No. 1, March 1967

PETER: I got introduced to the American Indian situation through Dave Ossman. One day he came into the studio and began to talk about the American Indian. I got very excited and I said, "where are they?" He said, "well, they're everywhere," and he began to talk about the Hopi. I said, "where are the Hopis," and he said, "they're in Arizona." So we decided to go to Arizona and do the Hopi, and that's how it started. The minute I made that decision, suddenly things began to appear. Craig Carpenter, who was a messenger for the traditional American Indian, was brought to me at the studio through a couple of people who heard over the show that we were interested in the Indians. And one Sunday night we took a lot of tapes of things he'd done in Hopi and a couple of years ago in the state of California, and studies Frank Waters did in Arizona and we cut them all up into a three hour show. It was our first Indian show — it caused a lot of comment — and from it came, as I say, people who would then put us in contact with others who were doing work, including Craig, and through that we got an invitation to go to Hopiland over Christmas.

What had happened was that back in October, I had gotten a reading, or I had been given the message actually, just through my head, that there was going to be an earthquake in San Francisco, not so much in Los Angeles, on the 26th of December at 2:00, and I decided at that time that I didn't want to be in Los Angeles when it hit and I went around telling people in the studio things like that. So we decided to go to Hopiland at that time. And sure enough at two in the afternoon on the 26th, there was an earthquake here. It was only a three point Richter instead of seven which I expected. I think the reason for that was we were in Hopiland at that time, praying like mad to cool it down here. That 3 or 4 days in Hopiland totally changed my head — totally.

For four days we lived inside the community and lived in the houses and talked with the people and walked around, and at first it was delightful, but after a while it became sort of awe-inspiring, for example, the day we took part in the prayer ceremony early in the morning. We arrived at four in the morning at one of the Indian's house. The ceremony didn't actually begin until around seven, so for three hours we sat in this room. There were maybe twenty of us — six or seven of us in our group, the Indians and their children . . . 3, 4, 5, 6, 7 years old . . . little kids. And not once during that time, that long extended period of quiet or at any time I was in Hopiland, did I hear one Indian child whine or bitch or nag.

TOM: Do you feel that the spirit of the Indian is being manifested through a lot of the young people today?

PETER: I'm very glad you asked that, because I had that in my mind. That's precisely how I feel. Not only that, I'll take it a little farther. I think the souls of Indians are coming back. I think they're coming back as the young people. I think it's a very valid explanation why suddenly, at a Be-In, you can see a couple of thousand people, not only dressed as Indians — not like costume — but in the spirit of Indian. It hit me all of a sudden. I started studying the Indian thing and doing the shows on it with no awareness whatsoever that there was a large segment of the community here and in San Francisco that were hip to it. You know, I thought it was very interesting and I'm particularly fascinated by it, and I do the shows for myself anyway. But then I go to the Be-In and I begin to see it. Now they're not wearing it like a costume, as I say. It's not a fad. It's not a clothing thing that can be copied in stores and such. It's mystical as hell. I don't know how they picked it up.

I offer for your fond inspection
Oz's bonafide protection
Against the forces dark & grim
That operate by law or whim
How sweet it is to know up front
That Fortune's cruel blade is blunt
And hardly fit
To stand against the Love-In kit

And so, if you be triply blessed,
Secure the button to your breast
Insure the card within your vest
Affix the sticker to your auto
Proclaiming joyfully our motto:

The vehicle is Ecstasy
The time is Now
The answer Yes ~

The
Wizard

OZ
Radio Free Oz
KPFK 90.7 fm

TEMPORARILY HUMBOLDT COUNTY
An American Pageant

First performed on the Columbia Records album
"Waiting For The Electrician, or Someone Like Him"
written and recorded by the Firesign Theatre,
Spring 1967.

All roles played by The Firesign Theatre

TEMPORARILY HUMBOLDT COUNTY
or, Manifest Destiny, Take 2

THE SCENE: AGAINST A BACKDROP OF THE PRAIRIES, TWO INDIANS IN FULL WARRIOR COSTUME AND MAKEUP WATCH AS A HERD OF BUFFALO PASS SLOWLY BY.

INDIAN: Well, I think it's about time. The way the corn's been growing for the last two generations . . .

2ND INDIAN: Look at that herd of buffalo! They're ready!

INDIAN: Everything's living the Great Spirit's Way — in Harmony.

2ND INDIAN: He'll be here soon.

INDIAN: The True While Brother is coming home. Remember what the Great Spirit said? If we did what we were supposed to do, and lived according to the Plan, White Brother would finish his work in the East and come back to us.

2ND INDIAN: It'll be nice to have the Family together again!

A CONQUISTADOR, A PADRE AND SEVERAL SPANISH SOLDIERS ENTER TO A TRUMPET FANFARE AND FLAMENCO MUSIC. THE BUFFALO SCATTER.

CONQUISTADOR: Buenos dias, amigos!

INDIAN: Hello! You must be the True White Brother!

CONQUISTADOR: Sure! You must be the Indians!

INDIAN: Yes!

2ND INDIAN: Welcome home!

ALL THE SPANISH SOLDIERS CHEER.

CONQUISTADOR: Welcome to New Spain! This is your new Father — Father Corona.

FATHER CORONA: (He's Irish!) Pax venuti nictum! Down on your knees, now! D'ye recognize what I'm holdin' over your heads, lads?

INDIAN: It's a Cross. The Symbol of the Quartering of the Universe into Active and Passive Principles.

FATHER CORONA: God have mercy on their heathen souls!

CONQUISTADOR: What the Father means is — what is the Cross made of? Gold! Have you got any?

INDIAN: No . . .

CONQUISTADOR: What about the Seven Cities of Gold? Phoenix? Tucson? Las Vegas?

2ND INDIAN: This is gold.

CONQUISTADOR: What's that?

INDIAN: Corn.

SPANISH SOLDIER: Corn! Now we can make tortillas!

2ND SPANISH SOLDIER: We've been waiting for this for hundreds of years!

3RD SPANISH SOLDIER: I just invented tacos!

CONQUISTADOR: So, is this all you've got?

INDIAN: Yes . . . but aren't you the True White Brother who's supposed to come and live with us in peace?

CONQUISTADOR:	Sure! Therefore, I claim this rich, verdant pasture land in the name of the Empire of Spain!
VESPUCCI:	(He's Italian!) Hey! Hey, Capitano! The rain, she's a-stoppa to fall! And the corn, she's all dead!
CONQUISTADOR:	Shudduppa' Vespucch'! I claim this stinking desert in the name of the Empire of Spain. Forever! Let's go!

THE SPANISH SOLDIERS GRUMBLE. THE BUFFALO HERD MILLS ABOUT.

SPANISH SOLDIERS:	(Singing) God bless Vespucciland, mmm-mmm-mmm . . .
FATHER CORONA:	Oh, by the way, Domini Domini Domini! You're all Catholics now! God bless you!
CONQUISTADOR:	Come on, Father. No one in their right mind would live in this stinking desert.
3RD SPANISH SOLDIER:	Come on, Cisco!

THE SPANIARDS LEAVE AND THE INDIANS HIDE AS A WAGON TRAIN ENTERS. ONE PIONEER PLAYS "OH, SUSANNA" ON HIS HARMONICA. ANOTHER PIONEER SPEAKS:

ANOTHER PIONEER:	Boy! I'm tired o' pushin' West. How long ago'd we leave Goshen?
3RD PIONEER:	'Bout two hours ago! Ain't we ever gonna stop?
PIONEER:	Quiet down now, boys. Wagon Boss is gonna speak!
WAGON BOSS:	My fellow settlers! We stand here at the Edge O' Civilization, on the banks of the Mississsouri River, lookin' West, at Our Destiny!
PIONEER:	You can say that again!

WAGON BOSS:	What may appear to the faint-hearted as a limitless expanse of Godforsaken wilderness . . .
3RD PIONEER:	Sure is!
WAGON BOSS:	. . . is, in reality, a Golden Opportunity for humble, God-fearin' people like ourselves, an' our families, an' our children, an' the generations a-comin', to carve a new life — outta the American Indian

THE INDIANS COME OUT OF HIDING.

INDIAN:	Welcome, White Brother!
WAGON BOSS:	Injuns! Draw the wagons up into a circle!
INDIAN:	Why do you always do that?
WAGON BOSS:	We git better reception that-a way. Mind if I put this antenna up on yonder peak?
2ND INDIAN:	That's our Sacred Mountain.
WAGON BOSS:	This is our Sacred Antenna! It's shaped like a cross. Made out of aluminum. Er — got any aluminum?
INDIAN:	We've still got some corn left.
PIONEER:	Hey! Corn! Now we can make whisky!
ANOTHER PIONEER:	We've been waitin' hundreds o' years fer this!
3RD PIONEER:	Say! I just invented a Tom Collins!
WAGON BOSS:	Here, Injun. Ya want some firewater?
INDIAN:	No. We were warned by our Elders not to drink anything that would make us weak or silly.
WAGON BOSS:	(Laughs) Put it in their well.

2ND INDIAN: That's not a well. It's the eye of the Holy Serpent Mound, on which you're standing.

WAGON BOSS: It's a beaut'!

INDIAN: No, it's a mound.

WAGON BOSS: And right purty, too! Er — can ya move it?

INDIAN: But, why?

WAGON BOSS: Railroad's comin' though! Right now!

A RAILROAD TRAIN LOADED WITH COWBOYS AND RAILROADERS PULLS IN. THE BUFFALO ARE SCATTERED AND THE HERD IS SPLIT.

COWBOY: Hey! What're we stoppin' fer?

RAILROADER: Are we in Goshen yet?

CONDUCTOR: Cain't go no further. This here's Injun Territory!

GOVERNMENT AGENT: Well, then! It's Treaty Time!

A BRASS BAND ENTERS, PLAYING "HAIL TO THE CHIEF."

GOVERNMENT AGENT: My fellow Redskins! Speaking for the Great White Father in Washington and all the American People, let me say we respect you savages for your Native Ability to instantly Adapt and Survive in whatever Godforsaken wilderness we move you to. Out there. Sign here!

THE INDIANS SHRUG AND PUT "X"S ON THE PAPER.

RAILROADER: They did it!

ALL THE COWBOYS WHOOP AND HOLLER. THE TRAIN AND BRASS BAND LEAVE.

INDIAN: No reason to complain. It's not so bad out there. We still have our People and our Ceremonies and the Sun, Moon and Stars, and the Sand, and the Black Stuff coming out of the ground…

GOVERNMENT AGENT: Black Stuff comin' out of the ground?

TRAILBLAZER: Civilization, ho-oooooo!

A PASSEL OF SOONERS, DOGS, MODEL T'S AND DUST STORMS PASSES BY, LEAVING THE INDIANS ALONE. THE WIND BLOWS.

2ND INDIAN: It's nice out here in the desert. No rain, no crops, no White Brother.

A GREYHOUND TOUR BUS PULLS UP, STOPS AND THE PASSENGERS FILE OUT.

BUS DRIVER: All out for Fort Stinkin' Desert! Last Indian Reservation for two thousand miles. You got fifteen minutes, folks. Get 'em while you can!

SEVERAL SHOTS RING OUT.

BUS DRIVER: Get the Senator back in the bus!

THE SENATOR FIRES OFF MORE SHOTS AT THE INDIANS AS HE IS LED AWAY.

SENATOR: Godfrey Daniel! Pesky Redskins! Which way's Goshen?

TOURIST: Howdy, there, Colorful Replicas of America's Past! When is the exciting-in-its-primitive-splendor Snake Dance going to take place?

INDIAN: It's usually in August, but with our children off in Indian School, there's no one left to do the ceremonies.

EDDIE GETS OFF THE BUS.

EDDIE: Hiya, Pop! I'm home!

2ND INDIAN: Hello, Soaring Eagle! It's good to have you back from school!

EDDIE: Aw, come on! Call me Eddie. I'm an American now!

2ND INDIAN: What have they been teaching you?

EDDIE: Just what we need for a better life! French horn, Italian, water polo . . .

GOVERNMENT AGENT: Yes, at Custer Memorial Indian School, Eddie's one of our Prize Students. We're giving him away next week.

INDIAN: Oh, my White Brother.

A HIPPIE FREAK GETS OFF THE BUS.

FREAK: Hey, man! Don't let him bring you down, now. There's a lot of young people in this country, just like myself, who really know where the Indian's at. And don't worry. Soon we're all gonna be out here on the Reservation, livin' like Indians, 'n' dressin' like Indians and doin' all the simple, beautiful things that you Indians do. Hey — got any peyote?

RICH TOURIST: Say, how much is that necklace you're wearing?

LADY TOURIST: Does anybody here know how to do the War Dance?

TOURIST WITH CAMERA: Hold it! Smile!

RICH TOURIST: Isn't it amazing how they survive on this stinking desert?

LAUGHING TOURIST: Ya got any scalps?

TOURIST WITH CAMERA: Lemme get a shot of you and yer squaw.

RICH TOURIST: Let's see the War Dance!

LADY TOURIST: Let's see you dance!

TOURISTS:	Let's see the Dance! Dance! Dance! Dance! Dance!

MORE SHOTS RING OUT. THE INDIANS DANCE IN A CIRCLE.

BUS DRIVER:	OK! OK, folks! Fun's over! Back on the bus!
MOTHER:	Where's little Billy Joe?
FATHER:	He's in that run-down outhouse over there, Mamma.
INDIAN:	That's our Sun Altar.
GOVERNMENT AGENT:	Well, Injuns, just goes to show you there's an obvious need to conserve our Priceless National Heritage. The Government is turning your home into a National Monument!

THE MARCHING BAND GETS OFF THE BUS, PLAYING "AMERICA THE BEAUTIFUL." THE SENATOR FOLLOWS.

SENATOR:	It behooves me, 'pon this Historic Occasion, to dedicate the Stinkin' Desert National Historical Monument and Cobalt Testing Range!
TRAILBLAZER:	Civilization, ho-ooooooo!

AS THE INDIANS WATCH, THE COBALT BOMB GOES OFF. THE SOUND DIES AWAY AFTER A TIME, AND THE SMOKE CLEARS, REVEALING THE TWO INDIANS BACK ON HORSEBACK.

INDIAN:	Well, it's about time. There's been no corn growing for the last few generations. The buffalo's gone. There's no one left to live in harmony.
2ND INDIAN:	I wonder where we went wrong?
INDIAN:	Let's just keep to the Life Plan. Remember what the Great White Spirit said: "Follow the Peaceful Way." The True White Brother is bound to come.

AN ASSISTANT MOVIE DIRECTOR RUNS ON, YELLING THROUGH A MEGAPHONE.

ASST DIRECTOR: All right, Indians! Get ready!

A SECOND ASSISTANT FOLLOWS, WITH A CLAP-STICK.

2ND ASST: "Winning Of The West — The Massacre." Take four!

HE CLAPS THE CLAP-STICK TO START A TAKE.

INDIAN: Well, let's go . . .

HE AND THE 2ND INDIAN JOIN A DOZEN OTHERS, WAR-PAINTED, WHO RIDE UP BESIDE HIM. THEN THEY ALL GALLOP AWAY IN TO THE SUNSET, WHOOPING. THE DESERT WIND BLOWS . . .

W. C. FIELDS FOREVER

First performed on the Columbia Records album, "Waiting For The Electrician, or Someone Like Him," written by the Firesign Theatre and recorded, Spring 1967.

Phil Austin as Gabby

Peter Bergman as Toker, Dr. Tim

David Ossman as Mello Jello, Ranger, Lt. Baha'ind

Phil Proctor as Medium Rari, Chemosabe, Lover

W. C. FIELDS FOREVER

THE FORT STINKIN' DESERT WIND BECOMES A GIANT, RIGHTEOUS TOKE. THE TOKER, HOLDING THE HIT, SEZ:

TOKER: Hey, Baby! Welcome to the Lazy Om Magic Circle Dues Ranch and Collective Love Farm! Take your clothes off and come on in!

THE DISCIPLES: Om . . . Om . . . Range . . .

TOKER: Here! Let me lay a stick of sandalwood incense on you — made it out of my own sandals. No, no, no! Let me light it for you. (Takes a toke) Yeah! . . . Nah . . . Let me show you around the place . . . Oh! Wow! Hey, where'd all those little people with the melty hats and the walls . . . Hey, man, now that you're all down home and tribal and all that, I want to take you up to the Second Bardo and orient you. Here's our Good-Games-People-Play Room . . .

MELLO: Hello! My name is Mello Jello. I am the head of the Athletic Department. I head the Athletic Department! I am the Athletic Department Head! Here! OK, beginners, everybody into the Fourth Lotus Position!

THE DISCIPLES GROAN

MELLO: Oh, yes — that's very good. That's very good! Now, you are going to stay there until you reach true Enlightenment.

THE DINNER GONG RINGS OUT.

RARI: Come and bless it! Grubs! Grubs!

DISCIPLES: Aw, grubs again! Grumble, grumble . . .

TOKER: Let me turn you on to Medium Rari, our mystic Chef and Guru.

RARI: Welcome to my humble chuckwagon. While you are here, we will have everything from soup to nuts. Tonight we have Mushroom Soup and Betel Nuts. Here, have some grubs. Oh, they are tender baby ones, cooked over incense in holy corn oil — that's oil from the corns of holy men, known in your country as polyunsaturated ghee!

TO THE THEME FROM "WILLIAM TELL," THE RANGER AND TANTRIC GALLOP IN.

RANGER: Scalp 'em Tantric!

TANTRIC: Groovy, Chemosabe!

TO THE SOUND OF HORRIBLE RIPS AND TEARS, RANGER GALLOPS OFF.

RANGER: Hi-ho, Electric Blue, away!

THE THEME FADES AWAY.

GABBY: Aw, Ranger's on a bum trip again . . . Howdy, Brahmachari. I'm Gabby, your Sacred Cowboy. You know, this reminds me very little of the time my Guru sent me out to clean up the Karma in Artful Dodge City. I stumped into the Last Chant Saloon . . .

WE FLASHBACK TO THE SALOON, WHERE COWBOYS ARE DRUNKENLY HARMONIZING:

COWBOYS: (Sort of Singing) Paramahansa Yogananda, parlez-vous . . .

DRUNK COWBOY: Hey, give me some more of that Third Red Eye, barkeep!

BARKEEP: You've had it! That's your last chant, Cowboy! Out!

GABBY: There was a passel of them Theosophists at the bar, raisin' the Devil. Had Him about ten feet off the floor. I could tell by the red clay on his hooves and his black aura that he was up to no good, so I looked him straight in the eye and said, "Sam Pakoo, there ain't enough room in this Life Cycle for both of us!" Well, that little Devil up and challenged me to a game of ten-card Tarot, Pentacles wild. I seen him deal a High Priestess off the bottom of the deck, and then . . .

INTERRUPTING BOTH THE NARRATIVE AND THE FLASHBACK, AN ARMY REGIMENT MARCHES IN, HALTING ON COMMAND:

BAHA'IND: Column A, halt! Column B, halt!

GABBY: It's Left-tennant Baha'ind, of the Seventh Seal Calvary!

BAHA'IND: I need three men! One from Column A and two from Column B. Drop out!

GABBY: Howdy, Left-tennant Baha'ind. What's up?

BAHA'IND: We ain't! Got some more locoweed?

GABBY: Sure! Got some Road Apple Red right here.

BAHA'IND HAS A HUMUNGOUS TOKE OF THE RED, THEN:

BAHA'IND: Which way'd we go . . . ?

GABBY: You went thataway!

AND THEY DO, AT HIGH SPEED. OVER A SQUAWKY PA SPEAKER WE HEAR:

LOVER: There will be an out-of-sight mandatory Sunrise Light Show at the Main Desert at 5:48, Sidereal time, Lovers! That is all!

GABBY: Procession will be starting soon. Let's go pick up Tiny Doctor Tim and head into the Sunrise. Now, this here simple life-size replica of the Taj Mahal, made entirely out of oleomargerine, houses our Guru, Dr. Tim. Let's knock on the door and see if he's in.

HE KNOCKS, PRODUCING AN UGLY SUCKING, THWAPPING SOUND. THE DOOR OPENS.

GABBY: Howdy, Dr. Tim!

DR. TIM: (He's tripping) I just thought I'd drop out and say hello . . . Hello!

GABBY: Come back, Dr. Tim. We want to talk to you!

DR. TIM: Oh. Welcome to the Link of Spirited Guhuary — LSG! Wait a minute . . . Oh, well . . . another day, another green, blue, electric yellow dollar! Got anything to drink? Anything at all?

FATHER O'REALLY: And why is it you're drinkin', Timmy me boy?

DR. TIM: 'Cause it's bad for my hullabalootions. I get a chance to see things in real black-and-white. I despise Electric Pink!

GABBY: Dr. Tim is the Keeper of the Sacred Tablets.

DR. TIM: Yeah. Here, have a Tablet.

A NEARBY HORSE WHINNIES.

DR. TIM: Oh! Nice paisley horsey! Give the nice horsey some sugar cubes . . . !

THE HORSE EATS THE CUBES, AND HIS WHINNEY CHANGES INTO AN ELEPHANT'S TRUMPETING. HE RUNS OFF INSANELY.

GABBY: Well, Dr. Tim, everybody's gathered for the Daily Miracle. Here's your microphone.

DR. TIM: Ever since the Sun took LSD, it's been a fundamentally better Sun — more pink and green and Electric Blue. Let's hope it comes up again today.

DISCIPLES:	He's done it again . . . It's coming up . . . It's coming up!
DR. TIM:	Oh! It's paisley! Has anybody got anything for an Acid stomach?
LOVER:	Alright, group! It's time to meditate on the Pure White Light of Stupidity! Let's hear it for our Guru. One, two, three!
DISCIPLES:	Gee . . . You . . . Are . . . You . . .
LOVER:	I'm not at all happy with the Flashcard Section! Now, come on, you Freaks! Say the Word, and you'll be Free! Say the Word and be like Me! Say the Word I'm thinking of. Have you heard? The Word is . . .
DISCIPLES:	Love . . . Love . . . Love . . . Love . . .
LOVER:	That stinks!
DISCIPLES:	Love . . . Love . . .
LOVER:	Pee-You!
DISCIPLES:	Love . . . love . . .

AND EVERYTHING FADES AWAY, INTO THE SUNRISE.

LE TREINTE-HUIT CUNEGONDE

First performed on the Columbia Records album, "Waiting For The Electrician, or Someone Like Him," written by the Firesign Theatre and recorded, Spring 1967.

Phil Austin as Old Lady, Malcolm X John Lennon

Peter Bergman as Joe, Stopan Coolit

David Ossman as Benway, Mom, Announcer, Chinese Diplomat, Major Hitte

Phil Proctor as Larry, Super-tendant, Senator K, Russian Diplomat, Anthem Singer

LE TRENTE-HUIT CUNEGONDE

JOE AND LARRY ARE CRUISING DOWN SUNSET AT SUNRISE. THEY ARE THE LOVE POLICE, JUST DOING THEIR JOB.

JOE: Hey, Larry. Dig that chick.

LARRY: She's groovy.

JOE: Hey, man! Are you ready for that spade?

LARRY: Wow! He's groovy! All spades are groovy.

JOE: Dig that chick. She's groovy.

LARRY: Right! Hey . . . ! Dig that!

JOE: She's not groovy!

LARRY: Mmm-hmmm . . .

THE PAISLEY PATROL CAR SIRENS OVER TO THE CURB. THE COPS BRACE THE SUSPECT.

JOE: Peace, baby.

OLD LADY: You talkin' to me, man?

JOE: Sure, baby. Come on over here. I wanna do a thing with ya.

OLD LADY: You wanna roofer?

JOE: No, man.

OLD LADY: A reaper?

LARRY: Forget it.

OLD LADY: Ringer?

LARRY: Where's yer mini-skirt?

OLD LADY: I forgot it! Oh, I knew I shouldn't go out on the street . . .

JOE: Cool it, lady. Don't get uptight.

LARRY: Come over here in the light, so we can check yer body paint. . . . Hmmm . . . faded San Francisco Art Nouveau.

JOE: Sure. She must be an Oldie.

LARRY: Are you holding?

OLD LADY: Natch! Er, Jackson. Of course I'm holding. I've got it right. . . Ooooo! You took my stash from me! This is a frame-up!

LARRY: Dig, Joe. Aspirin.

JOE: Let's do her a favor. Phone her in.

OLD LADY: I tell ya, I took all the uppers! You wanna hear me rap? "I saw the best minds of my generation destroyed by madness! Starving, hysterical, naked . . . "

LARRY: Put her in the car.

JOE: Out-a-sight! Call her in to Dr. Benway.

BENWAY: (On the phone) Oldie-But-Goldie City. Benway here.

LARRY: (On the phone) Hey, Doc! Got one for re-grooving. Be right in.

BENWAY:	(Not on the phone) Groovy. (A door opens to loud rock music.) How's the Bluecadelic-Psyco-Raga-Rock Old Folks Dance Marathon doing?
ASSISTANT:	They're dropping like flies!

THE DOOR SLAMS, THE MUSIC IS GONE.

BENWAY:	Groovy . . .

THE PHONE RINGS.

BENWAY:	Oldie-But-Goldie . . .
SUPER:	(On the phone) Super-tendant of Schools here.
BENWAY:	Groovy.
SUPER:	Groovy. Hey, man, it's about your kid — Malcolm X John Lennon? He dropped in today.
BENWAY:	(Now on the phone) You mean . . .
SUPER:	Benway, your kid's a drop-in.
BENWAY:	(On the phone) It'll kill his mother . . .
SUPER:	(At home) I just talked to your father. He's groovy.
MALCOLM:	Yeah, I like Pop . . .
SUPER:	Well, then — baby! How come we found you in a classroom today? Why weren't you hanging out in the parking lot with the rest of the kids and teachers?
MALCOLM:	I don't smoke. Can I go now?
SUPER:	Yeah, do your thing. Hold it! Leave those books here!
MOM:	Malcolm X John Lennon? Come in and dig your Mother.
MALCOLM:	Aw, Mom, I can't now. I gotta do my homewor . . . I — I — I mean — I gotta go meet my connection.

MOM:	You can't fool me! You're in one of those underground study cells, aren't you?
MALCOLM:	No!
MOM:	It'll kill your father. I didn't breast-feed you for fourteen years for this! Come here, baby . . .
MALCOLM:	But, Mom, I'm not hungry . . .
MOM:	Straightnik! Do yourself a favor. Be groovy. Now sit down, turn on and tune in the TV.
MALCOLM:	But, Mom! I don't wanna watch television!
MOM:	Oh, you're so weird . . .

THE TV CLICKS ON (FOR THE FIRST TIME IN FIRESIGN HISTORY) AND WE'RE LIVE FROM DC.

ANNOUNCER:	And now, direct from the Paisley House on Capitol Hill, man, we take you to the Gathering of the Tribes, which is already in session . . .
SENATOR K:	Now, let me sock it to you, baby! It's clear, from these underground films shot in your bedroom by the Free Food and Drugged Administration, that you've been doling out unauthorized bread and water to a chick who lost her Free Food Card.
WITNESS:	But, Senator, baby! Like, she was starving!
SENATOR K:	Young man! That's her trip! Take him away for re-uh-grooving.
ANNOUNCER:	And now, ladies and gentlemen, the Paisley House on Capitol Hill — your spot for the best in food, fun and dancing — proudly presents the fastest-rising Interim Governmental Administration in the Western Hemisphere — the Cabinet of the United States of Being! From Rochester, New York, on lead guitar, the Secretary of Peace! On drums, the Secretary of Inner Self! On saxophone, the Secretary of States of

Consciousness! And here he is, ladies and gentlemen! The Expected! The Most High! Chief of the United States of Being! Stopan' Coolit!

COOLIT: Do you love me?

CABINET: Yes, we do!

COOLIT: On the birthday of the Founder of our Tribe, Sodom Clinton Power — the first to take our sacred oath, "if elected, I refuse to serve!" Pow! I come to present for your hippification, the first Treaty of World Peace! Some of you cats may recall the old days of the brownshoes, when there was war and fightin' and soldiers . . .

SENATOR K: Yes, those were un-groovy times.

COOLIT: Well, now, there's no mo' war any more! And no soldiers! Except for our brave boys, livin' their trip in Nigeria.

RUSSIAN DIPLOMAT: Mr. Chieftan! Representing the Young People's Soviet Sociable Respublik, it's a gas to sign this jazzy document. We too want peace. Of Nigeria . . .

CHINESE DIPLOMAT: Yesterday, a few million of us in the Hippie Republic of China met in my room to debate this question. We threw I Ching — out the window! We are now unanimous.

COOLIT: How sweet it is! Hey, Secretary of Peace, baby, what're we puttin' down in Nigeria?

SECRETARY: Major Hitte is on the screen now, with the daily up-front report.

IN THE FINAL CHANGE OF SCENE, WE ARE NOW INSIDE A B-29 BOMBER.

HITTE: Ciao, baby! This is Major Hitte in the cockpit of the Enola McLuan, flagship of the Seventh Airborne Peace Corps and Lending Library. We're now over the center of rebel resistance in Northern Nigeria and preparing to drop literature.

PILOT: Do the bomb-bay door thing.

BOMBARDIER: Bomb-bay doors swinging and open, baby.

PILOT: Groovy and out. Bombardier, it's your karma.

HITTE: We're almost ready to drop it. I can see the entire rebel force running out of their huts, looking up at the sky.

PILOT: Seven — fourteen — eleven — sixteen . . .

COPILOT: Lazy Star Dog . . .

NAVIGATOR: North by Northwest . . .

BOMBARDIER: Target ready. Books away!

HITTE: There they go! The literature is in a tight pattern. The rebels are beginning to scatter — but it's too late! On target! God, this is an awesome moment! The last stronghold of un-hip resistance is out-of-sight, under eight million hard-bound copies of "The Naked Lunch!" It's all over! We're coming home!

AS THE BOOKS SCREAM EARTHWARD, THE NATURAL ANTHEM RISES HEAVENWARD AND THE B-29 FLIES HOME.

ANTHEM SINGER: Ofay, are you hip
To the dawn's daily flash?
In the Ramparts we read,
We're so gallantly dreaming
And the Rockettes red hair . . .

FADE SLOWLY OUT.

A SHADOW MOVES UPON A LAND

Performed by The Firesign Theatre live at the Magic Mushroom and broadcast on KRLA-AM, November 26, 1967

Written by Phil Austin

A SHADOW MOVES UPON A LAND

DAVID: The Firesign Theatre presents — A SHADOW MOVES UPON A LAND.

MODERATE SPEED, BUILD SLOWLY TO CLIMAX

PHIL A: For I remember stopping by the way
To watch a Potter thumping his wet clay
And with its all-obliterated tongue
It murmured "Gently, Brother, gently, pray!"

DAVID: A dreadfully fatal intermittent fever broke out in the lower parts of this river about eleven weeks ago.

PHIL P: In the month of August the intermittent fever began to shake its burning, freezing subjects.

PETER: Prior to the year 1830, when the ague and fever was not known to exist.

PHIL A: The epidemic ague, which has swept away great numbers of the natives, commenced in 1830.

PETER: ...was not known to exist.

DAVID: The main disorder is an intermittent fever which has carried off all or nearly all the Indians.

PHIL P: Since the year 1829, probably seven-eighths have been swept away by disease, principally by fever and ague.

PETER: The fever and ague was never known in this country before the year 1829.

PHIL A:	...prior to the year 1830, when the ague and fever was not known to exist.
PETER:	...was never known in this country before the year 1829.
PHIL A:	...was not known to exist

BUILD, BUILD

DAVID:	In 1829 attacked by fever, attended with ague...
PHIL P:	The intermittent fever has appeared at this place.
PETER:	There are a great many Indians here at present, some few of them have the ague.
PHIL A:	On the Sacramento River, we are informed by the Indians that they have no traditions of any similar scourge in past time.
DAVID:	There appears to be some sickness prevailing among them, resembling an ague.
PHIL P:	...when the ague and fever was not known to exist.
PHIL A:	We are informed by the Indians that they have no traditions of any similar scourge in past time.
PETER:	The fever and ague was never known in this country before the year 1829.
PHIL A:	...no traditions of any similar scourge in past time
PHIL P:	...was not known to exist
PHIL A:	...they have no traditions of any similar scourge
PHIL P:	...was not known to exist
PETER:	...never known in this country.
PHIL P:	...was not known to exist.

PHIL A: ...no traditions

CLIMAX AND LONG PAUSE — THEN START SLOWLY AND METHODICALLY

DAVID: Since 1829 an intermittent fever has carried off vast numbers of the Indians.

PHIL P: The symptoms are a general coldness, soreness and stiffness of the limbs and body with violent tertian ague. Its fatal termination is attributable to its tendency to attack the liver.

PETER: The Indians of the Columbia were once a numerous and powerful people; the shore of the river, for scores of miles, was lined with their villages.

PHIL A: Upwards of a hundred individuals were writhing in agony on the floors of the houses

START TO BUILD QUICKLY

DAVID: I have found the Indian population in the lower country below the falls of the Columbia, far less than I had expected. Since the year 1829

PHIL P: 1829

DAVID: 1829, probably seven-eights have been swept away by disease.

PETER: So many and so sudden were the deaths which occurred that the shores were strewn with the unburied dead.

PHIL A: Whole and large villages were depopulated and some entire tribes have disappeared.

PHIL P: The intermittent fever has appeared at this place and carried off *three-fourths* of the Indian population.

DAVID: The Multnomah Indians have become as a tribe extinct —

(PAUSE)
The Multnomah Indians have become as a tribe extinct
(PAUSE)
As a tribe extinct
(PAUSE)

NOW, KIDDIES, VERY GENTLY, MODERATE SPEED AND THEN SLOW IT DOWN

PHIL P:	The shores of the river were strewn with the dead and dying.
PETER:	For only a few years since, they numbered upwards of a hundred while now they are said to be less than thirty.
PHIL A:	The fever and ague have swept off the whole tribe.
DAVID:	Some Some sickness prevails among the Indians on the Feather River. Some sickness prevails among the Indians on the Feather River. The villages which were so populous when we passed that way in January now seem almost deserted and have a desolate appearance.
PHIL P:	The few wretched Indians who remain are lying apparently unable to move. It is not starvation It is not starvation as they have considerable quantities of their winter stock of acorns remaining.
PETER:	The natives along here seem even more wretched than those on the Feather River, the villages seem almost wholly depopulated.
PHIL A:	The fever and ague was never known in this country before 1829.
PHIL P:	The unhappy wretches are found in ones or twos in little thickets of bushes

	The unhappy wretches are found in ones or twos in little thickets of bushes
DAVID:	Some sickness prevails among the Indians on the Feather River.
PHIL P:	Only two women are left
	The Indians are all dead, only two women are left
DAVID:	As a tribe extinct
PETER:	To have nearly become extinct in consequence.
PHIL A:	The fever and ague was never known in this country before 1829.

PAUSE — TRANSITION — THEN SLOWLY BUT WITH ENERGY

DAVID: On the whole, our available information gives the impression that the mortality ran somewhere between 40 and 100 percent. The latter value is undoubtedly excessive, although to be sure, the incidence, as opposed to the mortality, may well have reached that figure. 40 percent seems too low. At this point it will be remembered that the evidence pertaining to the malaria epidemic

malaria epidemic

malaria epidemic on the Columbia River indicated a mortality among the Indians of approximately 75 percent. Since all the circumstances were very similar in the two regions being considered, and since what California data we have support rather than disclaim the conclusion, we may set the mortality in California at the same value as for Oregon, that is 75 percent.

that is, 75 percent.

that is

PHIL P:	The unhappy wretches are found in ones or twos in little thickets of bushes
DAVID:	...75 percent.
PHIL A:	...we are informed by the Indians that they have no traditions of any similar scourge in past time.
DAVID:	This is a startling and disturbing result. It means that fully twenty thousand natives of the great Central Valley died in 1833; my own opinion is that this figure is too small. It means that three-quarters three-quarters of the Indians who had resisted seventy years of Mexican and Spanish domination were wiped out in one summer it means that the red race in the heart of California was so crippled that it could offer but the shadow of opposition to the gold-mining flood which swept over it in 1849.
PHIL A:	...We are informed by the Indians that they have no traditions of any similar scourge in past time.
PETER:	...The fever and ague was never known in this country before the year 1829.
PHIL P:	...prior to the year 1830, when the ague and fever, or any disease resembling it, was not known to exist.
DAVID:	...malaria epidemic
SLOWING	
PHIL A:	...we are informed by the Indians that they have no traditions of any similar scourge in past time.
PHIL P:	...The unhappy wretches are found in ones or twos in little thickets of bushes
DAVID:	...that is, 75 percent

PHIL A:	...We are informed by the Indians
MUSIC:	BEATLES "GETTING BETTER"
PHIL A:	In the beginning, there was no beginning. They made up beginnings later to prove to themselves that it *was* later. If every later had been a now, there would have been no excuse.
DAVID:	Let me say right now that they have lied to us. They have led us to believe that we are children only of time, that our stay, our dwelling-time on this, our world, has been infinitesimal. See, they say, how much farther we may go.
PHIL A:	They say that we rose from and above the animals.
DAVID:	They lie — animals are former friends, to whom we no longer speak.
PHIL A:	We chose not to speak when the Ram carried the high, looping message which crackled with divine fire between his horns in the airless mystery of manifestation; and upon touching the pentacle, grounded that fire, leaving the message split, perceivable, transferable...
DAVID:	Show me the myth, the legend, the superstition of any of the old people which says one day an ape stood up and said he was a man.
PHIL A:	They have lied to us — told us not to listen to the old people, the old memories:
PETER:	The word myth:
PHIL P:	Judgment — a story to explain the sun
PETER:	It is not true.
PHIL P:	The word legend:
PETER:	Judgment — an inauthentic story handed down by tradition

PHIL P:	It is not true.
PHIL A:	So there we were, all of us, and someone said hey, a bull has two horns; this vegetative, flowering, seasonal bull that we are and we live in and that's standing right over there has two horns. The brothers, the north-south brothers who pummel the divine message through the pentacle, theirs was not division, it was only two. As the Ram and the Bull had only carried the hint of two, the signal, as it were (and two, let's face it, is not a bad idea) the north-south war gods, crackling their fire, dancing through the earth, *made* two — connected, point to point and back again, and then white brother split for the East and that made three.
	Man, his white brother in the East and the promise between them — the promise that appeared and vanished like a Holy Ghost — that made three. And then one day White Brother forgot and became White Man and that made four and that's where the trouble started. That remembrance, that holy remembrance, that recognition, that smile, that hello, it's you again is it?, that never happened. That hasn't happened yet, now, could happen, any time now, one second from now, past and always here, the effort, the tiny effort, look at him and say, hello, it's you again is it? Again, again, say hello again and we can stop messing around and get on with it. It hasn't happened yet.
	White man, Red brother, the promise remembered and the promise forgotten — that made four. Welcome crab, goodbye four-leggeds. Search for the moon.
CROSS-FADE TO:	
MUSIC:	BEATLES "THE WORD"
PHIL A:	The history of the White Man in what he calls America, when seen from the standpoint of what he calls the Indian, is complex at best. For an Indian to detail that history would be even more invidious a task than composing a chronicle of the moon; it would be analogous to writing a complete history of the locusts.

DAVE: Consider a history of the Locusts, running to several volumes, with names and dates and an analysis, an analytical tour de force, that would make the movements of individual locusts, properly named and set down by their markings, or tribes or whatever, comprehensible to the reader. Consider merely the problem of the coming of the locusts. From the great historical viewpoint, was it merely the nature of the locust to come, to devour? When the Locust tells you with wide-eyed innocence that he came for freedom, or for gold, or to escape some peculiarly locustian religious pogrom, do you believe him? Or do you lay his rampages to the mindless strivings of individual locusts, when it's so hard to tell one locust from another?

PHIL A: And when the battles have been already lost and gone and the locust has imprisoned your children in his schools, and killed the bulk of your people by fire and sword and disease and unkindness, when the locust cries in his milk about the pollution of his God-given rivers, where do you begin? How do you set down the men and women who, when the killing of the two-leggeds and four-leggeds had reduced the splendid ecology of this land to nothingness, came to your grandfathers and told them they were dirty, that they were to be reserved for something that they seemed to have forgotten, who called themselves Superintendents and Matrons and Colonels and Mistresses and Masters and who turned your children by force and greed from the land and did a remarkably good job of almost making them locusts?

DAVID: Lower Echelon Locusts. Fruit-pickers, telephone repairmen, maids in the Locustian homes of Omaha and Tacoma and Buffalo.

CHANT:

PHIL A: Everybody now knows Indians are good.

DAVID: Everybody now knows Indians are good.

PETER: Everybody now knows Indians are good.

PHIL P:	Indians, Indians, good, good, good.
PHIL A:	My country 'tis of thee
DAVID:	Boo!
PETER:	The sentiment, young man, you just expressed Will find no home within my breast
PHIL P:	For we have found it to be true
DAVID:	White men are bad and Indians true blue.
PHIL A:	Well, folks, upon hearing this, I was pretty amazed and I looked down at my skin and sure enough it was white.
DAVID:	White as snow.
PETER:	White as ice.
PHIL P:	White as terror.
PHIL A:	Well. I could see that these fellas know where it was at, and besides they'd read Moby Dick, and I decided to throw myself at the feet of the Oracle.
DAVID:	So to speak.
PETER:	The American Indian
PHIL A:	they said
PHIL P:	is the perfect embodiment of the holiness of the human condition.
DAVID:	The American Indian
PHIL A:	they said
PETER:	has many alternatives to offer to our way of life.
PHIL P:	The American Indian

PHIL A:	they said
DAVID:	is where it's at.
PHIL A:	I was fired up. My blood boiled at the thought of the wrongs to the Indian done. I thought with relish of his ceremonies, of this fine and noble religion and I thought and thought, and smoked and smoked, until I flashed upon what I, we, all of us could do to remedy the wrongs of the ages.

SINGING, TO "HEAT WAVE":

PHIL P:	Oh —
PHIL A:	we're —
PHILS:	Havin' a love-in
D & P:	Coo coo ca choo
PHILS:	A loveable love-in
D & P:	Coo coo ca choo
PHIL P:	Our temperature's risin'
PHIL A:	It won't be surprisin'
PHIL P:	When we're in the Grand
ALL:	Can-yon!
PHIL A:	We'll have the Jefferson Airplane
DAVID:	And the Grateful Dead
PETER:	The scenery's perfect
PHIL P:	Just right for a head
PHIL A:	We'll get The Who and Jimi Hendrix

DAVID:	And we'll fly out the Fugs
PETER:	Hey does anybody know if the Grand Canyon's got any electrical plugs?
PHIL P:	Well,
PHIL A:	then...
PHIL P:	Let's see —
PHIL A:	Let's go out — and see the —
ALL:	Hopi!
PHIL A:	Bu doo bop deedle diddy (ETC. — 4 BARS)
SOUND:	KNOCK — WIND — KNOCK
DAVID:	Hello.
PHIL P:	Hi Indian brother, we're your soul brothers from the cities, re-establishing our connection with the land and its peoples.
PETER:	And we're planning a love-in.
DAVID:	A what?
PHIL A:	A loveable love-in
PHIL P:	in the Grand Canyon
PETER:	and we thought you might like to come
PHIL A:	since it's in your honor.
DAVID:	Well...
PHIL P:	And we wondered if you maybe had a long extension cord.
DAVID:	But...

PETER:	And maybe you could bring along some food to feed the people
PHIL A:	since it's in your honor.
DAVID:	It's going to be a hard summer, no rain. If we don't dance and pray all summer and tend the corn there will be no food. I don't think so. No.
PHILS & PETER:	No?!
PETER:	Whaddya mean no? Do you realize, Indian Brother of mine, that the Grand Canyon is the property of the people?
PHIL P:	And we are the people?
DAVID:	No. Why can't you just leave us alone.
PHIL A:	Leave you alone? My God, man, don't you realize what's happening? It's us, us, your friends.
PETER:	Your day has come.
PHIL P:	You're known.
PHIL A:	You're understood.
PETER:	You're hip.
PHIL P:	You're on the cover of the Oracle
PHIL A:	the Free Press
PETER:	Cheetah Magazine
PHIL P:	the KRLA Beat
PHIL A:	Monkee Teen
PETER:	the East Village Other
PHIL P:	the Evergreen Review

PHIL A:	Open City
PETER:	the Saturday Evening Post
PHIL P:	Life
PHIL A:	Time
PETER:	Fortune
PHIL P:	the Wall Street Journal
PHIL A:	Rapture
PETER:	Keyhole
PHIL P:	Leather Thighs
PHIL A:	Eff You, A Magazine Of The Arts
PETER:	Don't you see, my brother? We've got a lot invested in you.
PHIL P:	And if you don't pay off
PHIL A:	We'll look like fools
PETER:	to the readers of the
PHIL P:	Oracle Free Press Cheetah
PHIL A:	Beat Monkee Teen
PETER:	EVO EVR FU
PHIL P:	Don't you see?
DAVID:	I see.
ALL:	You see?
DAVID:	I see. Nice try. You've done it again.

ALL.	We've done it again!
DAVID:	You've done it again. You can't help it, I suppose. Living where you live and thinking what you think. I suppose you can't help it. I suppose *none of you* can help it. I suppose none of you *could* help it. I suppose you couldn't help it at Jamestown, at the Trail of Tears, at Council Bluffs, at the Little Big Horn, at Wounded Knee. I suppose you couldn't help the Nez Perce, the Ojibwa, the Cree, the Cahuilla, the Apache. I suppose you couldn't help the treaties. I suppose you *can't* just let us alone. We're like a toy for you to play with. Goodbye.
(SILENCE)	
PETER:	Well, I guess it's back to the negroes.
SINGING:	
PHIL P:	Oh —
PHIL A:	we're —
PHILS:	Havin' a Festival
PETER:	Coo coo ca choo
PHILS:	An angry Arts Festival
PETER:	Coo coo ca choo
PHILS:	Weeeeeeeee love you, weeeeeeeee —
PETER & DAVID:	Coo coo ca choo
PHILS:	(HARMONIZING) Loooooove you...
PHIL A:	There is a Shoshone boy now imprisoned by the United States Army for three years, because he refused to go to Vietnam. His defense rested, and we assume the appeals will also, on one very simple point. The point is so simple, so glaringly simple, that it will probably be turned into a funny television series someday.

DAVID:	The Shoshone nation, you see, is a foreign country. It was recognized by the United States Government as such in all the treaties. And the young man fails to see why he, as a member of a foreign nation, should go to Vietnam to do to the Vietnamese what the White Man has done to his people. The United States Government tells him he's a citizen of the U.S. It's like conferring honorary citizenship on the French and then drafting their young men.
PETER:	It's a funny idea, Harry. You see, there's this tribe of Indians...
PHIL P:	I'm dying with laughter already!
PETER:	And this tribe of Indians decide they're not a part of the U.S. anymore.
PHIL P:	That's a little far-fetched ain't it?
PETER:	It doesn't matter, it's funny, isn't it?
PHIL P:	A scream!
PETER:	Okay, can't you see it? Edward Everett Horton as a Polish Indian and Leo G. Carroll as the phony Medicine Man...
PHIL P:	I'm dying with laughter!
DAVID:	What is it about this country? About this thing called White Man? White Man is an adjectival distinction describing a human being of any race, creed or color who finds it impossible to leave nature or man alone. White Man is he who must control, must fight the elements.
PHIL A:	And don't tell me with pride of King Lear battling hurricanes and waterspouts. He was mad on the heath, and what's more, very unhappy. It is the condition of White Man to be unhappy, because what he tries to do is patently impossible. The Indians could tell him how to live. They're very helpful that way. What's left of them.

DAVID:	Pennacook
PHIL P:	Massachusett
PETER:	Mohegan
PHIL A:	Delaware
DAVID:	Mohawk
PHIL P:	Powhatan
PETER:	Alabama
PHIL A:	Cree
DAVID:	Choctaw
PHIL P:	Tuscarora
PETER:	Susquehanna
PHIL A:	Iroquois
DAVID:	Pennacook Massachusett Mohegan Delaware
PHIL P:	Mohawk Powhatan Alabama Cree
PETER:	Choctaw Tuscarora Susquehanna Iroquois
PHIL A:	Chickasaw Chickasaw
DAVID:	Sauk Sans Arc Shawnee
PHIL A:	Arapahoe Arapahoe
PHIL P:	Crow Oto Iowa
PHIL A:	Menominee Menominee
PETER:	Mandan Mobile Modoc

A CHANT — EACH LINE ENTERS THEN REPEATS

DAVID:	Hopi	Apache	Nisqually	Shoshone
PHIL P:	Apache	Nisqually	Shoshone	Hopi
PETER:	Nisqually	Shoshone	Hopi	Apache
PHIL A:	Shoshone	Hopi	Apache	Nisqually

REPEAT AND BUILD

PHIL A: Paiute Paiute Paiute

DAVID: In a sacred manner you shall walk
Your nation shall behold you

PHIL A: Chickasaw

PHIL P: Sauk Sans Arc Shawnee

DAVID: Behold! A sacred voice is calling you.
All over the sky a sacred voice is calling

PHIL A: Chickasaw

PETER: Sauk Sans Arc Shawnee

DAVID: In a sacred manner you shall walk
Your nation shall behold you.

MUSIC: BEATLES "GOOD DAY SUNSHINE"

FREEK FOR A WEEK!

Performed live at the Magic Mushroom, broadcast on KRLA-AM, December 10, 1967

Phil Austin as Billy

Peter Bergman as Jerry, Roy, Kunkin, Goozik, Uncle Tom

David Ossman as Ken, Gnat, Acapulco, Dad

Phil Proctor as Gene, Ralph, Garcia, Shiv, Tommy

FREEK FOR A WEEK!

THERE IS NO PREPARATION WHATEVER BEFORE A NICELY-DRESSED TELEVISION ANNOUNCER (KEN) COMES ON STAGE AND UP TO A MICROPHONE. THE HOUSE LIGHTS REMAIN UP.

KEN: Good evening, ladies and gentlemen. Well, this is the first time for many of you and naturally, being here is a little different than watching the show at home. Well, in the minute or so we have before we go on, I'd just like to ask you to feel comfortable. Roy and Gene are out there with you now, helping to create the atmosphere that will show the folks at home that we're having a lot of fun! How are you doing out there, boys?

ROY AND GENE HAVE ENTERED THE HOUSE AND ARE SPRAYING THE AUDIENCE FROM OLD-FASHIONED "FLIT GUNS." THEY ARE MASKED AND MUMBLE AND WAVE.

KEN: I'd just like to tell you one little story about our favorite fella — Jerry Yarrow. Seems he was having himself a weekend off, up in Vegas, naturally, and he met himself a real looker of a showgirl at the Dunes. Well, old Jerry decided he'd like to paint the young lady in the nude! But, unfortunately, she made him put his clothes back on! OK! Say, Roy and Gene! Are you all finished?

ROY: We're all ready!

GENE: And they are too!

ROY AND GENE COME UP ON STAGE.

KEN: All right, ladies and gentlemen! The air is charged with excitement and expectancy and with about 5,000 cc's of a powerful and well-beloved hallucinogen. So, in just ten seconds, you'll all be ready to play "This Is Your Trip!" Quiet, now . . . stand by . . .

AFTER A FEW SECONDS, THE LIGHTS COME UP ON STAGE AND GO OUT ON THE HOUSE. A BIG MUSIC THEME STRIKES UP.

KEN: Good evening, Mr. and Mrs. America! Once again it's Tuesday night and time to play America's favorite game, "This Is Your Trip!" And here he is — your smiling, genial host — the man who made "ego-death" a household word — it's Jerry Yarrow!

JERRY: High there! What's happening? Thank you, Ken, and thank you, too, in our lovely studio audience! Well, I know what's happening — we're ready to play "Truth or Schizophrenia!" (He sniffs the air) Ah! There's still some out there, so let's open up our lungs and take a big, deep breath for Jerry. Ready now? One, two, three, breathe! (He holds his breath) Come on, now! That lovely grandmother — I can see by your corsage that it must be your birthday — come on now! Breathe it in, gran'ma. You'll love it when it happens! (He lets his breath out)

KEN AND GENE, APPEARING IN A SMALL ADVERTISING SET, WITH THE PRODUCT.

KEN: For you folks at home who want to play along with our studio audience, be sure and pick up a Jerry Yarrow Aerosol Bomb — available in Family . . .

GENE: And Tribe Size.

KEN: And then you'll know. . .

GENE and KEN: What's happening!

KEN: Jerry . . .

JERRY: Thank you, Ken. We're ready for our first contestant — but is he ready for us? While Ken is down in the studio audience picking him out, here's a word from our first sponsor, Ralph Spoilsport of Ralph Spoilsport Motors in the City of Encino . . .

KEN GOES INTO THE AUDIENCE, LOOKING FOR A LIKELY CONTESTANT AND THE SHOW CUTS AWAY TO A LIVE COMMERCIAL FROM A USED CAR LOT.

RALPH: Hiya, friends! Ralph Spoilsport, Ralph Spoilsport Motors, here at the world's largest new-used and used-new automobile dealership — Ralph Spoilsport Motors — in the city of Eczema. Well, friends, as you probably know, we're overstocked again in all makes and models — every conceivable license plate — here, at the greatest show on earth! All the new tinplates — the '69s, the 70's, the ultramodern '72s — not to mention the greatest stockpile ever of completely used automobiles and mountains of spare parts in our mammoth showrooms — here at Ralph Spoilsport Motors, in the City of Emphysema! Let's take a look at just a few of these fabulous deals! Birch's Blacklist says this car, an all-new, brand-new used 1958 NARC-60! This car is supposed to sell for *25-hundred* dollars, tax included with proper improval of bank credit . . . our price to you, including chrome inside and outside trim, two-way sneeze-through windvents, brass brushings, fenderents, edible sponge-coated steering column, and interior design by Frederick's of Hollywood! Our complete price? Only two-thousand *five-hundred* dollars, in easy monthly payments of 25 dollars a week, twice a week and never on Sunday! So come on down and see us! We'll be glad to talk to you personally. And remember — we're open now and every day, except today, so hop in your car and head in any direction on the freeway of your choice, because all freeways and every channel leads to Ralph Spoilsport Motors — the world's biggest — Ralph Spoilsport Motors in the City of Debt. Thanks for the interruption and now back to our movie . . .

RETURNING TO THE TV SHOW, JERRY IS ON STAGE AND KEN, WITH BILLY FROM THE AUDIENCE MOVE TO JOIN HIM.

JERRY:	What's happening?
KEN:	I've got one, Jerry!
JERRY:	Well, good! Bring him up — if he isn't already!

A NICE, BOUNCY BIT OF THEME MUSIC BRINGS BILLY TO THE MIKE.

JERRY:	Hello there, son. What's your name and where are you from?
BILLY:	Billy Artunian, and I'm from Fresno.
JERRY:	Fresno! Well, Freddy, what brings you to Pasadena?
BILLY:	I came to Los Angeles to visit my mother. She's in the hospital in Inglewood. She's got this thing on her liver . . .
JERRY:	Oh, really?
BILLY:	Yeah, well, we don't expect her to live very long.
JERRY:	Well, isn't she a good sport anyway, folks? And so are you, Billy. You look to me like you're ready to play "You Bet Your Karma!"
BILLY:	What is it?
JERRY:	Oh, you're not familiar with the simple rules of our little game?
BILLY:	No, I'm not.
JERRY:	Well, boys — let's turn him on!

KEN AND GENE STEP OUT TO EITHER SIDE OF BILLY, ARMED WITH BUG SPRAYERS.

BILLY:	What's happening?
JERRY:	Exactly, Billy. Now, don't worry, because all these hallucinogens have been prepared under the constant

scrutiny and supervision of the Armenian Medical Association. Boys — give him the Sacrament!

ACCOMPANIED BY A BIG MUSICAL CHORD, THE "BOYS" SPRAY BILLY WITH A FINE MIST.

BILLY: I don't feel a thing.

JERRY: Billy may not feel anything now, folks, but he will!

BILLY TURNS AND ALMOST WALKS OFF STAGE BEFORE KEN STOPS HIM AND BRINGS HIM BACK.

JERRY: Oooooo! Isn't he going to be surprised!

BILLY TURNS THE OTHER WAY AND ALMOST GETS OFF STAGE BEFORE GENE BRINGS HIM BACK. BILLY MUMBLES THROUGHOUT.

BILLY: Gee, it's hot in here . . . I'm cold . . . Is there anything to eat . . . ? I'd like an orange . . . or the Sun . . .

JERRY: The rules of our little game are very simple, Freddy. You have from now until the end of the show to realize your True Self and discover the Key to a Better Universe!

BILLY: Wow!

BILLY IS IN THE FIRST STAGE OF HIS ACID TRIP. IT'S ALL SO STRANGE AND WEIRD!

JERRY: He's knocking at the door to Bardo One! It's happening! Where's he going to go? Will he make it? Here's Ken and Gene to kick him off with a Trip through Reality. Careful now — he's just like a baby . . .

GENE AND KEN SURROUND BILLY.

KEN: Walk! Don't Walk! Walk! Don't Walk! Walk! (etc.)

GENE: Tennhutt! Pull in your gut! Stick out your chest! Stick out your tongue! You've got cancer! Keep your hands off yourself! Your fingernails are filthy! Don't slouch!

When are you gonna get a haircut? When are you gonna do your homework? When are you gonna get a job? When are you gonna get a car? When are you gonna get a girl? When are you gonna get a nose-job? HUP! Two three four! Hup! Two three four . . .

THEY CONTINUE THIS TORTURE, BUILDING IT TO A CLIMAX, UNTIL BILLY STOPS WRITHING AND STANDS TRANSFIXED.

JERRY: This is it! He's on the threshold of Bardo One! Is it Happening? Where's he going to go? Is he a winner or a loser?

A BIG MUSICAL CHORD!

BILLY: I'm dropping out of here!

JERRY: He's dropping out! He's a winner, folks! He's reached Bardo One and he's ready to try for Bardo Two!

BILLY: I'm dropping out! Dropping . . . dropping! I dropped out . . . I'm a free man! It's wonderful! It's easy! Why isn't everybody free? I want to share my Experience! I'm going to open a temple . . . an ashram . . . a Center . . . a Store! And I'll sell the things that make people truly free — old military uniforms, lava lamps, roach holders, Frank Zappa posters! Yeah!

HE'S THERE. THE STORE IS REAL. THE LITTLE TINKLY DOORBELL RINGS.

BILLY: Peace, love and flowers! Blow your mind at the Tripsville Drugstore!

GNAT COMES IN AND LOOKS AROUND.

GNAT: Wow, Mr. Artunian! You have the most beautiful psycho doolic shop in the whole world! It's so big . . .

BILLY: Give the people blacklight and they shall be free.

GNAT: But — are you really getting to the people?

BILLY:	What? Of course I'm getting to the people! I sold a million Frank Zappa sitting-on-the-toilet posters last year.
GNAT:	They want more!
BILLY:	I'll get them more. They only cost me fifty cents a thousand.
GNAT:	But they want things that will stimulate their minds.
BILLY:	Have you seen my lava lamps?
GNAT:	No. I mean — intellectually stimulating!
BILLY:	Just look at this poster of Albert Einstein making out with Joan Baez . . .
GNAT:	No . . . what I'm talking about is the power of the Written Word. You see, five years ago, I had this flash — about a magazine! A magazine that frees people!
BILLY:	I like that.
GNAT:	See — this is the magazine that tells the Truth! And I've gone without food, or a place to crash, just to do the research. And I got the best artists and real melty type, and this day-glo picture of me and Gloria . . .
BILLY:	What's it called?
GNAT:	UTE.
BILLY:	UTE?
GNAT:	Right!
BILLY:	Wonderful! I like it! The freedom of the American Indian . . . UTE . . .
GNAT:	No! That's U. T. E. — Up The Establishment!
BILLY:	I like that even better!

GNAT:	I've invested everything I've got, and all the bread my family's got, and that my friend's got — but I'm still short $187 to get out the first issue.
BILLY:	$187? Well, you've got it!
GNAT:	Oh, Mr. Artunian!
BILLY:	I'll take 80 percent of the magazine, all post-publication rights, and you can sleep in the back!
GNAT:	Where's the back?

GNAT LEAVES IN THAT DIRECTION AND THE PHONE RINGS. BILLY ANSWERS IT.

BILLY:	UTE Magazine and Allied Industries, up yours! . . . The AC-DC March for Exposure? Just a minute, I'll have one of my boys cover it. Kunkin!

KUNKIN ENTERS, A LOT LIKE STEPIN FETCHIT.

KUNKIN:	Yassah, boss!
BILLY:	Gate A at Oak and Elm. Take along the psychadoolic camera and get me some out-of-focus brutality for page one!
KUNKIN:	Yassah, boss!

HE EXITS AND GARCIA ENTERS, CARRYING A PHOTOGRAPH.

GARCIA:	Hey, Chief! Take that Love-In off the front page! I got a scoop that's gonna blow the lid off from under the country!
BILLY:	What is it, Garcia?
GARCIA:	Look at this picture. What do you see?
BILLY:	It's a bush.
GARCIA:	Right, boss! But look behind the bush!

BILLY:	You mean that series of random dots?
GARCIA:	Right, chief! That's the last of the 36-man tag-team that assassinated the President! And look what he's got in his hand!
BILLY:	A bush?
GARCIA:	No! It's not a bush! That's a 114-millimeter Finnish anti-tank gun!
BILLY:	Oh, Garcia! You don't believe in that 114-mm Finnish anti-tank gun single-shell theory, do you?
GARCIA:	OK, Chief! If you don't believe me, take the words of your own eyes. Look at this blowup!
BILLY:	It's a random series of giant dots holding a bush.
GARCIA:	Squint, Chief!
BILLY:	By God, you're right, Garcia!
GARCIA:	You see him? You see the assassin?
BILLY:	It's Hubert Humphrey!
GARCIA:	Right, Chief! The one man who had nothing to gain and he gained nothing.
BILLY:	Get cracking!
GARCIA:	No, he wasn't anywhere near there . . .
BILLY:	Get Humphrey, then!
GARCIA:	OK, Chief! Up the Establishment!

GARCIA LEAVES, MEETING GOOZICK AND GOLDSTEEN AT THE DOOR. THEY ARE UNSAVORY CHARACTERS.

BILLY:	Peace, love and flowers. Come on in.

GOOZICK: Is dis UTE Magazine?

BILLY: Yes.

GOOZICK: I'm from de Syndicate!

BILLY: De Syndicate?

GOOZICK: De Underground Press Syndicate.

BILLY: You must be Herman "The Flower Child" Goozick.

GOOZICK: De very same. You are obviously acquainted with my Karma. I should like for you to cohabit with my friend and accountant, Irving "Acapulco" Goldsteen.

BILLY: How do you do?

GOOZICK: Dis is a nice little business you got here. I should hate to have to send around the Original Diggers to rearrange your wallpaper!

BILLY: Is that a threat?

GOOZICK: Don't be paranoid! It's just dat Acapulco here tells me that you don't respond so good to the poster inviting you to join de Syndicate.

BILLY: I thought it was a rock group.

ACAPULCO: It is — only we don't play.

GOOZICK: You remember what happened at the Oracle?

BILLY: Yeah, somebody broke in in the middle of the day and threw acid on the art director. You can't scare me! I've seen "Bonnie and Clyde!" I'm not afraid of Death!

GOOZICK: Shaddup! You may have experienced ego-death, but body-death is something else!

AT THIS MOMENT, AN EVEN MORE DANGEROUS CHARACTER ENTERS THE SHOP — IT'S THE CRYSTAL SHIV.

BILLY: My God! It's the Crystal Shiv!

GOOZICK: You want maybe I should let him strap a monkey on you back?

SHIV: Let me shoot him up, Boss!

BILLY: I just don't see what the Syndicate has to offer.

GOOZICK: Freedom from body-death for openers.

SHIV: Let me open him!

GOOZICK: Shaddup! Plus that, you get the friendly and harmonious cooperation of the other members of the Syndicate! Such as . . .

ACAPULCO: The L. A. Free Press, The Village Voice and the Boikley Barbituate.

BILLY: I own them all.

GOOZICK: Look Magazine?

BILLY: I'm in negotiation.

GOOZICK: OK, wise guy! So you won't play ball, huh? Me and the boys are gonna have a little confrontation . . .

THE THREE GOONS HUDDLE. THEY BREAK.

GOOZICK: All right! We'll sleep in the back!

AND OFF THEY GO. BILLY WANDERS UP AND DOWN, LOST IN HIS DREAM.

BILLY: Wow! Here I am! It's all mine. I own all the Frank Zappa posters in the world. All the lava lamps. All the roach holders. All the fancy Spanish cigarette papers that come apart in your mouth. All the underground newspapers. All the *newspapers*! I own it all! Everything! And it all means nothing! To me! Because I killed my Ego! I did it! Me! Number One! I'm alright,

Jack! Mr. Clean! No Ego on this boy! Move aside, World! Here comes No Ego, Baby!

WHILE HE'S SPEAKING, JERRY COMES ON AND LISTENS. THEN:

JERRY: He's done it! It's happening! He's killed his Ego and he's out of Bardo Two!

A BIG MUSIC CHORD MARKS THE MOMENT.

JERRY: Now! The final test. Bardo Three, farther than any contestant has ever gone! Is it too big for him? Can he handle it?

BILLY: Wow! I can see for miles and miles and miles!

JERRY: What's it all for, Billy? Can you tell us?

BILLY: I can see that all the money and all the power I have is only good for one thing . . .

JERRY: No prompting from the audience, now.

BILLY: To bring peace and happiness to this troubled world, and solve the problems of mankind!

JERRY: I think he's going to make it!

BILLY: I'll pool all my resources. Material wealth doesn't mean anything anyway. And I'll share with everybody. Let's see now — I'll need a world-wide organization, so I'll hire . . . no, I'll offer jobs . . . no . . . I'll get my friends to help . . . Wait a minute! What am I doing? How did I get so involved? So attached? Who am I kidding? I never dropped out. But it's not too late to do it. Or not to do it. Or to stop fooling myself with plans. Or no plans. I can do it! It's up to me to do it! All I have to do is Lov . . .

WHILE BILLY IS PASSING ON TO THE NEXT BARDO, JERRY HAS INDICATED TO KEN THAT HE SHOULD CUT THE CONTESTANT'S MICROPHONE AND READ A COMMERCIAL. AT THIS MOMENT, BILLY'S MIKE IS CUT.

JERRY: Well! While our contestant is deliberating, let's hear a quick word from this week's alternate sponsor — Fantastic Cigarettes!

ON A SEPARATE SET, AN ANNOUNCER HOLDS UP A CIGARETTE. SOME JUMPY COMMERCIAL MUSIC BEHIND.

ANNOUNCER: Fantastic! Fantastic Cigarettes! Longer, longer, longer! Smoother, smoother, smoother! A rare blend of Armenian and Algerian tobaccos. Fantastic! The Cigarette that smokes itself . . .

A STRANGE HAND EMERGES AND LIGHTS THE CIGARETTE, WHICH SPARKLES.

ANNOUNCER: Fantastic! (He giggles.)

THE MUSIC AND CIGARETTE BOTH GO OUT. JERRY IS BACK FRONT AND CENTER.

JERRY: What's happening! (Confidentially) Well, have we ever got a surprise! Unbeknownst to our contestant, we've brought Billy's father all the way from Artunianopolis —and he's waiting just off stage in our airtight room. Ken is bringing him in before he suffocates. (Aloud) We've got a special treat for you, Ernie . . . and here he comes now! It's your Dad!

KEN USHERS DAD IN, ALONG WITH UNCLE TOM. A BIT OF "OH, MEIN PAPA" ON THEIR ENTRANCE. BILLY'S MIKE COMES ON SUDDENLY, FINDING HIM JUST WHERE HE WAS.

BILLY: . . . ove! It's so simple!

DAD: Hello, son.

BILLY: Gee, Dad! Hello, sir. Dad — I'm truly dropping out. I'm giving it all up.

DAD: You mean you want to cut your hair and give up your multi-billion dollar industries? That shows a lot of courage and imagination, and I think it's wonderful. So does your Uncle Tom from the World Bank of Fresno.

Right, Tom?

TOM: Right as rain, Walter. Some of the greatest men in the history of our country have had short hair.

DAD: And here's your little brother Tommy — he's Captain of the team now . . .

TOMMY ENTERS LIKE A CHEERLEADER.

TOMMY: Hell! No! We won't go! Right, Chucko?

BILLY: Gee, it's wonderful you see it my way.

DAD: We do, son. We do. We only wish that the thousands of fine Americans who work for you down in Frank Zappa Poster City could see it your way.

BILLY: Well, I'm not responsible . . .

UNCLE TOM: No, you're not responsible. But don't you realize that Artunian Amalgamated is responsible — for 58.4 percent of the National Gross Product. 58.4 percent. Just want you to think about that, son.

DAD: We just want you to think about that, son.

TOMMY: We just want you to think about that, son.

BILLY: Gee, Dad, Uncle Tom . . . don't you see that all that is meaningless? What's important is . . .

TOMMY: But, gee, Chucko! What about my summer job? What am I gonna tell the guys on the team? They were all gonna work for me, when I was gonna work for you! How can I show my face in the locker room?

BILLY: Gee, kid — I didn't realize . . .

DAD: You see, son — no man is an island . . .

TOMMY: Yeah, Chucko! It's like the Coach says — do unto others as you would do unto them. You know?

UNCLE TOM: You see, boy, there comes a time in every mature man's life when he has to ask himself "What's happening!" What's happening?

TOMMY: What's happening?

DAD: What's happening, son?

BILLY: Gee, dad — I guess you're right. I just wanted to make people free. But I guess it's not that easy.

DAD: No, it's not, son.

BILLY: Well, maybe I don't have to give it all up. Maybe it is possible to do some good . . .

UNCLE TOM: Of course it is, son.

BILLY: I could help the handicapped . . . feed the starving . . . be eyes for the blind . . . I'll need a world-wide organization, of course . . .

TOMMY: I'll work for you, Chucko!

DURING BILLY'S NEXT SPEECH, THE "FAMILY" RETURNS IN THEIR ORIGINAL CHARACTERS.

BILLY: We can do it! I can do it! All I have to do is face reality! But slowly — it can't all be done at once! It may not even be accomplished in my lifetime. But I see a bright vision of the future. I see the promise of Tomorrow! A world with no hunger, no disease, no poverty, no hangups! I can make it happen! I can change the world!

JERRY: What? Did I hear right? Did he say it? Did he really say it, Ken?

KEN: Yes, he did, Jerry!

GENE BRINGS IN THE ACID HEAD ROBE AND CROWN AND A HUGE BOUQUET OF FLOWERS. THE MUSIC HAS THAT FAMILIAR "THERE SHE GOES" FEEL.

JERRY:	He's realized his True Self and found the Key to a Better Universe! He's over the top of Bardo Three, and that makes him our Winner! Bill Artunian of Fresno, California, you're our Freek For A Week!
GENE (SINGING):	There he goes! Mr. Acid Head! There he goes! What a freek! His consciousness expanded, his awareness has grown — now his all-American mind is blown! There he is, walking on air he is! Freek For A Weeek he is! Mr. Acid Head!

THE MUSIC PLAYS ON AS JERRY GIVES THE CLOSING ANNOUNCEMENT.

JERRY:	This has been "Freek For A Week," brought to you this week and every week by Ralph Spoilsport and Fantastic Cigarettes. Be with us again tomorrow, when another unsuspecting contestant will take the wackiest and most dangerous trip of all — the search for self-realization! Until then, this is Jerry Yarrow, thanking you for being such a lovely audience, and for letting us expand your consciousness just a little. So, goodbye until tomorrow, when I'll ask you once again, What's Happening?????

THE SONG ENDS, THE STAGE PICTURE FREEZES, KEN GIVES THE "CUT" SIGNAL AND THE LIGHTS GO OUT.

PROFILES IN BARBEQUE SAUCE
The Convention of Ought '68

Performed live at the Kaleidoscope and at the
Ashgrove on March 24, 1968.
LBJ withdrew a few days later,
Dr. King was killed April 4th and
RFK on June 4th.
(It was a bad year. Think of the real Democratic
Convention in Chicago.)

All parts played by The Firesign Theatre.

PROFILES IN BARBEQUE SAUCE

A SUDDEN BLACKOUT. A FUZZY OLD 16MM MOVIE SOUNDTRACK BLARES OUT:

NARRATOR: 10 — 9 — 8 — 7 — 6 — 5 — 4 — 3 — SOUND — START . . .

THEME MUSIC PLAYS FROM A SLOW START.

NARRATOR: Urpee Classroom Films presents Educational Series 142 — "Adventures in Democracy in Action."

MUSIC COMES UP AND FADES OUT UNDER THE SCENE.

STROBE LIGHTS CREATE A STILTED "MOVIE" ACTION. WE SEE DAD, PASTING BLUE CHIP STAMPS INTO A BOOKLET. HIS SON ENTERS.

SON: Hiya, Dad!

THE SEQUENCE REVERSES AND THEN REPEATS, ALONG WITH THE MUSIC. AS THE ACTION REPEATS, THE STROBE EFFECT STOPS.

SON: Hiya, Dad.

DAD: Hello, Ronnie.

SON: Mind if I talk to you for a minute, sir?

DAD: Of course not, son. I'm almost finished here. (He rips a stamp off his tongue) I can see something's troubling you.

SON:	My American Supremacy teacher assigned me this dumb paper on Democracy, and I'm supposed to play doctor with Bruce.
DAD:	Just a minute, Eddie. You couldn't call Democracy dumb if you knew as much about America as Mr. Brown, down at the World Bank of Fresno knows.
SON:	But, Dad — that's you.
DAD:	Affirmative, Bobby. (He sticks a stamp on SON'S forehead. SON salutes.) Sit down, Son. In order to understand the workings of our Democratic Society, you have to familiarize yourself with the American System of Checks and Balances.
SON:	Oh, I know about that! You write the check and the Bank of America keeps the balances.
DAD:	Negative, Joey! (He rips off the stamp.)
SON:	Ouch!
DAD:	I'm talking about the delicate balance among the Three Branches of our Government — The Executive, The Presidency, and The White House.

A LARGE PIE CHART APPEARS, INDICATING THE BRANCHES.

SON:	Gee! Did we always have a Tripartite Form of Government, Doctor?
DAD:	No, Bruce. We had to fight for it. This country is built on the bodies of Young Men like yourself, who paid the Price of Freedom with their lives in order to die in Peace.
SON:	Oh — you mean the Indians?
DAD:	Nyet, Terry! (He rips off the SON'S nose) I'm speaking of Patriots like young Hamilton Alexander, who was hanged for his belief that all men should live in Liberty and Justice . . .

"CROSSFADE" TO ALEXANDER, A NOOSE AROUND HIS NECK, WRITING A LETTER. HIS VOICE FADES OVER DAD'S.

ALEXANDER: . . . live in Liberty and Justice, Dottie. And not under the Oppressive Thumb. Even in these last lingering seconds of my life, my Darling, my thoughts fly back to the Future of out Fledgling State, which now must rest in the hands of Ben, and Tom, and Gouvenour Morris, the latter of whom, Ben tells me, in his letter of the 6th, escorted you to that last stormy meeting of the Continental Congress. Which prompts me to ask, my Dearest One, what the Hell were you doing with Gouvenour Morr . . . aaggggg . . .

HE IS HUNG AND AFTER HE HANGS WE CROSSFADE BACK TO DAD AND SON.

SON: Gee whiz!

DAD: You see, Son? That first Continental Congress was the prototype of our present-day Nominating Conventions — the very heartbeat of the Body Politick. I'll never forget the Convention of Ought '68 . . .

SON: Wow! That was right before the End of the World.

DAD: As we know it, Arnie. It all took place in Munich, Illinois — in a beer hall not much bigger than this one. As a matter of fact, it was this one . . .

SON: Gee, Dad — it must've been Hell in there!

DAD LAUGHS AND THE TWO OF THEM LEAVE THE STAGE TO BILLY SHEERS, WHO ENTERS AND RAPS FOR ORDER ON THE PODIUM.

BILLY: Thank you, Gouvenour Morris, for that stirring benediction! And he's raised a few interesting points, which I would like to respond to all in my good time! I may have only been three years old at the time of the Hungarian Revolution, but I opposed its conclusion then as I support its opposition now! And I shall continue to do so, as long as the present Administration breaks every Treaty, undermines every effort toward honest confrontation and throws evey international agreement out the window and over the dam — which is bursting daily in the face of World Opinion! And if this makes me a so-called Negro in your eyes, then it's high-time we made the choice between Aunt Jemima and Uncle Sam!! And they tell you not to get so emotional. Well then, what the fuck is there to get emotional about??? I think that answers my charges pretty well. I'm only here for one reason and you're only here for one reason, too — that's to hear the man who's got all the answers that nobody else has! And he's had them for a long time! A former Postmaster General, the oldest living member of the New Left, and one hell of a Fighting Liberal — Harrison B. "Billy" Mossbach!

THERE IS A LOUD DEMONSTRATION FOR BILLY BY A PERSON IN THE AUDIENCE AS THE OLD LEFTY ENTERS.

BILLY: Young people all over the World — and I include Youth in Asia! I am no more afraid to watch you burn your draft cards than I am to send you off to war. They tell us — and they shall remain nameless only so long as you allow them to remain nameless, by any other name — they tell us that lightning cannot strike twice at the same time — in the same place. But I tell you that at this very moment, American ships of War are dropping millions of munitions on the playing fields of French Indo China. A glance at any National Geographic should convince any of you — and would do you all a lot of good!

A MAN IN THE CROWD STANDS.

MAN: But what about the obvious?

BILLY: We're not here to discuss the obvious — sit down — because I'd rather see my sons popping glue, pills, than shooting up — Vietnamese — Cong — and there ain't no use to sit and wonder why, Babe! Make no mistake — we cannot stand behind these faceless few who turn their backs and refuse to face the issue. Let us not lose face! Rather let us back to the hilt them that sides with us from behind! . . . Thank you. And now I open the floor to Nominees for the Next President of these United States of America!

ANOTHER MAN IN THE AUDIENCE SPEAKS. HE HAS NO MICROPHONE, BUT HE SIMULATES ONE BREAKING UP, ON AND OFF, FINALLY ON.

ANOTHER MAN: (Finally) The proud state of Texico, where oil wells that end well — Yahoo! — is proud to place in nomination its only living Son, the now and future King, President Lyndon Baines Caesar!

AN ENORMOUS DEMONSTRATION, FLASHBULBS AND COWBELLS, AS LBC ENTERS FROM THE REAR. PRESIDENTIAL MUSIC PLAYS AS HE COMES DOWN THE AISLE, SHAKING HANDS AND AD LIBBING . . .

LBC: Where the hell is Hubert, god damn it! . . . What're you lookin' at, boy? . . .

AS LBC GETS TO THE STAGE, THE MUSIC AND DEMONSTRATION QUIETS ALMOST COMPLETELY. TWO NETWORK CORRESPONDENTS APPEAR AT A NEARBY DESK.

WALTER: Well, Chet — according to our IBM projection, the demonstration will go on for at least 27 minutes.

CHET: Right, Walter. And I might remind you that 27, Theosophically reduced is 9, and that's the card of the Hermit and the House of Images. Can I have my deck back?

WALTER: Sure. And, as a Virgo, the President couldn't have picked a better day to accept the Presidency. Pluto has just moved into the House of White, which bodes Death in Automobiles to any opposition.

CHET: Just a moment, Walter. We've been ordered to return to the floor for the Inaugural Address. Harry . . .

THE MUSIC COMES TO A BIG ENDING AND THERE'S A FINAL CHEER.

LBC: My fellow Merkins! Faced as we are with Grave

Domestic Problems at Home and Gravier International Problems Abroad, there are Forces within my Country that dare to say that the continual drain of our Manhood is a risk too hard for us to bear. Well, it is hard. But, my friends, we will stick it out! (A big CHEER) What are our problems? We face fundamentally only four in number — all great, but none greater than the other. One is The War. Two is the Armed Conflict in Asia. Three is the Military Aggression in the Far East. Four is the Escalation of Hostilities from the North. Not to mention The Plague.

RFK HAS BEEN IN THE AUDIENCE ALL ALONG, DISGUISED AS THE DEMONSTRATION. AT THIS POINT HE REVEALS HIMSELF.

RFK: Mr. President! Mr. President, what about The Plague?

LBC: I told you not to mention that!

WITHOUT A SECOND THOUGHT, LBC PULLS OUT A COWBOY GUN AND SHOOTS RFK. SS MEN RUSH UP AND SHOOT RFK, WHO FALLS IN THE AISLE.

LBC: (Demonstrating) Look. Only one bullet. One bullet.

WITH THAT, LBC LEAVES THE STAGE, ACCOMPANIED BY ONE SS MAN. THE SECOND ONE ("TED") GOES UP TO THE MICROPHONE.

TED: And now, everybody — here he is! The man who made jurisprudence a household myth, your smiling, senile host — Earl "Mr. Justice" Warren!

A BIG TV THEME BRINGS EARL TO THE MIKE.

EARL: Whaaaaat happened? Well, while Ted is down on the floor looking for the Victim, I'll explain the simple rules of "Whodunit." In order to determine the identity of the Assassin, the Victim, chosen from the audience, will have the opportunity to ask three questions — one to each of our three Mystery Suspects. To which they must respond with the Truth, the Whole Truth and Nothing But the Truth, so help them God! Ted? Are you ready with our Victim?

TED IS DRAGGING RFK'S BODY UP THE AISLE.

TED: Yes! We're got one, Earl!

EARL: Let's put him On The Spot!

TO MORE THEME MUSIC, TED BRINGS RFK ON STAGE, DAUBS BLOOD ON HIM AND SITS HIM IN A CHAIR.

TED: Are you comfortable, Senator?

RFK: Could someone bind my wounds, please?

EARL: No time for that, because we're ready to play "Whodunit." Would you ask your first question of Suspect Number One?

SUSPECT #1 IS LBC.

RFK: Number One, where were you and what were you doing when I was shot down?

EARL: I'm sorry, but that was two questions. You're only allowed one per suspect. Will you rephrase it, please.

RFK: Let me say this — where were you when I was murdered?

LBC: I was attending my Convention at the time, and if I recollect rightly, so was you.

EARL: The Victim and Suspect Number One were in the same room. He had the opportunity. Now, Suspect Number Two.

ONCE AGAIN, THE SUSPECT IS LBC.

RFK: Number Two, what were you doing at the time this crime was committed against me?

LBC: I was responding in righteous indignation to your challenge from the floor.

EARL: The Victim had challenged Suspect Number Two. He had a motive.

RFK: Mr. Warren, at this time, I would like to enter this object as an exhibit.

EARL: All right, Victim. This object is a 45-caliber Smith & Wesson dum-dum bullet, still tainted with poisonous barbecue sauce. I'll accept it as Exhibit A and put it in the Archives for 99 years. You may ask your third and final question of Suspect Number Three.

NO SURPRISE HERE, IT'S LBC.

RFK: Number Three, did you ever see that bullet before?

LBC: Yes. I remember loading it into my gun just before my Inaugural Address.

EARL: He had the Victim's murder bullet. All right, Victim, that's all the questions you have. The time has come for you to make your choice and tell us "Whodunit." Was it Suspect Number One, Two or Three?

A SUSPENSE THEME PLAYS AS RFK DECIDES.

RFK: Suspect Number Two.

EARL: You're . . . wrong!

A BIG NASTY BUZZER SOUNDS.

EARL: Number Two did indeed have the motive, but he did not have the opportunity, as did Suspect Number One, nor the murder bullet, as did Suspect Number Three. Only one man was at the scene of the crime, and provoked the attack, and was in possession of the murder bullet. That man was . . . you — the Victim! You assassinated yourself!

WRAP-UP MUSIC COMES IN AS EARL CONTINUES.

EARL: And now, the time we've all been waiting for! When the fickle finger of Justice points to you and you alone must pay your debt to Society for the heinous crime of suicide. We'll be back with the Execution in just a minute, but first . . .

EARL AND TED ARE GONE. THE SCENE CHANGES TO THE FAMILIAR FATHER AND SON, AS LBC SPEAKS TO RFK.

LBC: Well, Bobby, before you become the greatest sacrifice any father can make for his country, I'd like to know if I've helped you form any new insights into the workings of Democracy in Action.

RFK: Gee, no, Dad. I don't think I'm ever going to finish that dumb paper. Everything's gone dark.

LBC TURNS AWAY FROM RFK AND DOES A COMMERCIAL.

LBC: The same thing happened to me many times when I was Majority Leader. The slightest little crisis would put me right to sleep. Then Lady Bug turned me on to an Old Texas Remedy — a simple little pill called Methedrine. The red, white and blue spansule that keeps America on the go-go. Try one, son, and you'll see . . .

WHEN LBC TURNS BACK TO RFK, HE SEES THAT RFK HAS LEFT THE STAGE.

LBC: The fuck . . . ?

HE LEAVES, FURIOUS. WE'RE NOW BACK WITH THE NETWORK CORRESPONDENTS.

WALTER: We interrupt this commercial to bring you a special program. Direct from the LBC Television Network Newsroom in New York — Election Eve, Ought '68!

CHET: This is it, Walter. We'll be here through the evening, reporting the fastest and most accurate returns of what promises to be the most unusual election in the colorful history of American politics.

WALTER:	That's true, Chet. The first returns from New Hampshire are dribbling in, and our ICBM computer is digesting them, so we ought to have the first prostheses in (he listens to his earpiece) about three minutes.
CHET:	Well, that gives us time to rerun the tape of the speech which has set the tone for this Election Day. If we can run that right now . . .

LBC APPEARS TO BE IN THE OVAL OFFICE.

LBC:	My fellow Merkins. This morning, at 3 a.m., with the advice and consent of my wife and my doctor, I personally declared total war on the hostile forces which oppose us in the North. At this very moment, my fellow Merkins, our entire Air Strike Command, led by my daughter in Air Force One, are dropping millions of tons of red-hot jellied barbeque sauce on the Port of Hyanis.

LBC DISAPPEARS AND THE CORRESPONDENTS RETURN.

WALTER:	Well, Chet, that was the high-point of the President's message and, as everyone knows by now, Senator Kennedy's victory hopes in the largely industrial New England basin were destroyed.
CHET:	Along, of course, with New England. Informed sources close to Sen. Kennedy report that he survived that initial attack and is now feverishly campaigning on the West Coast. Speaking of fever, Walter, what is the latest report on the Plague?
WALTER:	As you can see by the map, the President's bacteriological attack at Noon today, on the Headquarters of Kennedy's running-mate, the late Sen. McCarthy, was only partly successful. The saturation of Minneapolis-St. Paul with contaminated pork sausage, while apparently failing to stop Kennedy, has effectively spread the Plague clear to the West Coast, as shown by the scarlet lines on the map.

CHET: Not any more, Walter. We can rule out California and most of the Western States as a hiding place for Kennedy, because this report, just coming through now, confirms earlier rumors that the area west of the Rocky Mountains has fallen into the sea, which puts it pretty squarely into the Johnson camp.

WALTER: Chet — our transmission lines through to the President's campaign headquarters at Camp Ranch have been restored and we'll go there now, for a Special Report. Sandy?

ANOTHER REPORTER DOES A STAND-UP AT THE RANCH.

SANDY: Camp is the word for what's happening back at the Ranch. The President is surrounded by his many staunch supporters as he stands in an open barbeque pit, glistening with hog fat and glory, shaking hands with his trusted campaign managers — General Wallace, General Ky, General Rap Brown, General Franco, Mrs. Walter Brennan, General Ho, General Duke Wayne and Vice President Nixon. The feeling here at Camp Ranch is that ultimate victory is not far away. Press Secretary Chandler promises that Sen. Kennedy will soon be run to ground. Further proof that the end is near is . . . oh, wait a minute! There's a tremendous commotion over there as two Boy Scouts bring in something — some sort of a present — it's — it's the head of Sen. McCarthy on a . . . Well, Chet — a cheer has gone up from the crowd as the President puts on his barbeque apron and . . .

CHET: Excuse me, Sandy, but we'll have to interrupt your report now.

SANDY: That's all right with me, Chet. Oh, God . . .

STAND-UP SANDY RUNS OFF TO BE SICK AND WE CUT BACK.

CHET: While Sandy was on the air from Camp Ranch, we've received the significant news that the President has been successful in the Midwest and the South.

WALTER: That's right, Chet. His latest grass-roots offensive has carried the day. The Marines have laid down a thin layer of hog-fat across the twenty-five remaining states and have ignited it.

CHET: That pretty effectively wraps it up, Walter. All that remains is the state of Texas and the Island of Manhattan. Senator Kennedy's body has not yet been identified — or have we some further word on that, Charles?

WE HEAR "CHARLES'" VOICE. IT IS RFK.

RFK: Ah, no, I believe he's still at large.

WALTER: Well, that's the way it is. So now the President-reelect, with what's left of the country squarely behind him, faces the truly American challenge of draining our rivers and lakes of barbeque sauce and reclaiming our purple mountains and fruited plains from the locusts, frogs and boils. And that's the news from Election Central, today, March 24, 'ought '68. Good night, Chet.

CHET: Good night, Walter.

AS THE LIGHTS FADE, THE CLATTERY MOVIE NARRATOR VOICE RETURNS, ALONG WITH THE URPEE THEME MUSIC.

NARRATOR: This has been Urpee Classroom Films Number 142 — Adventures in Democracy in Action. Any similarity to persons dying or dead is purely Presidential.

THE MUSIC CROSSFADES TO A MARIACHI VERSION OF "GOD BLESS AMERICA" AS THE HOUSE LIGHTS COME UP.

BULK RATE
U.S. POSTAGE
PAID
PERMIT NO. 1491
PASADENA,
CALIF. 91101

ald
1101
=
TED

ALL THE NEWS THATS FUN TO PRINT

The Ice House Herald

A'S FEBRUARY FLING

RD

STEVE MARTIN
Comedy, magic and banjo. An Encore engagement for an engaging personality.

THE FIRESIGN THEATRE
A wild comedy quartet in the modern vein. Comments on surprising things. For comedy lovers. Featuring Peter Bergman, of Radio Free Oz, Philip Austin, Philip Proctor, David Ossman An "in happening" and a new, smash act.

February 13 - 25

CLABE HANGAN
Good old folk music and solid talent.

The Firesign Theatre Opens at the Ice House
Los Angeles Times, Wed. Feb. 21, 1968

The Firesign Theatre, appearing at the Ice House, Pasadena, through Sunday is the most refreshing comedy act to appear in many a moon (which they stole in their first skit opening night).

Better catch it from the top, or you'll think you checked your sanity at the door. The quartet (are there only four?) combine writing and acting talents with a ferocious zest and split-hair timing.

Not a show for relaxation, the fast delivery requires full attention. The opening show was very long and overloaded with humor. This philosophical satire was rather like a second desert after a heavy meal.

NITERY REVIEWS — Pasadena Ice House
Variety, Thurs. Feb 15, 1968

A wild, way out satire of Sherlock Holmes highlighted opening of two-week bill Tuesday (13) and seems to fit this type spot. However, in a standard nitery it would be out of place.

Quartet gets off some clever lines, but overall theme of the famed English detective looking for the culprit who stole the moon becomes a little too far-fetched and ridiculous. All are equally adept in portraying the various characters throughout the 30-minute playlet, slipping back and forth from behind a wall flat and sputtering the lines in rapid-fire fashion.

The habitués here reacted to all the dialogue, even when it just hung in midair, and at the conclusion accorded the foursome heavy applause. For an encore, group did a five-minute hit on Cowboys and Indians, giving it a contemporary racist switch by leaving with a "What's it all about, public?"

THANKSGIVING,
Or, Pass The Indian Please

Written by Phil Austin

Performed by The Firesign Theatre as an encore for performances from 1968 to 2011, this voice-poem began as a part of Austin's "A Shadow Moves Upon A Land" (inserted right before The Beatles "The Word"). It premiered on stage at the Pasadena Ice House, February 16, 1968

THANKSGIVING,
Or, Pass The Indian Please

PETER: Ladies and Gentlemen! The Firesign County Unified School District is proud to present

PHIL P: for your edification

PETER: the down-right awe-inspiring, never-before witnessed Historical Pageant:

PHIL P: Thanksgiving, or

PETER: Pass the Indian, Please, or

PHIL A: Thanksgiving, or

DAVID: None of the Above!

PHIL A: Over there we have some settlers and pilgrims and merchants and trappers all dressed funny in funny hats and buckly shoes and the soldiers in armor.

PETER & PHIL P: Just folks!

PHIL P: And on that side, we have some Indians, all dressed up and looking like Currier and Ives.

DAVID & PHIL A: Guardians of this sacred land.

PETER: In between, this bounteous feast, untouched as yet by hand of man.

ALL: Yum, yum!

DAVID: The leader of the White Man speaks:

PETER:	Let's whop them Indians!
PHIL A:	He says.
DAVID:	We Indians, as usual not saying anything,
PHIL A:	Don't say nothing.
PHIL P:	A typical scene, folks. One which will be repeated thousands of times
PETER:	In the thousands of times
PHIL P:	to come.
PHIL A:	Except!
PETER:	This first one was different.
PHIL P:	Why did this first one have to be different?
DAVID:	It didn't seem different at first.
PHIL A:	One of the soldiers walked over to one of the Indians and throttled him.
DAVID:	Aaaggg!
PHIL A:	Well, you can bet that made the folks in the buckly shoes proud as punch.
PETER:	Manifest Destiny!
DAVID:	said the captain of the ship.
PHIL P:	That Indian is good and dead!
PHIL A:	said the minister's wife.
PETER:	A dead Indian is good!
DAVID:	countered the dragoon.

PHIL P:	The only good Indian is a dead Indian!
PHIL A:	cleverly rejoined a little boy.
DAVID:	And they all applauded!
ALL:	APPLAUSE
PHIL A:	And they were going to let the little boy eat the Indian's heart —
PHIL P:	Yum, yum!
DAVID:	When someone,
PHIL A:	I think it was the minister,
DAVID:	Remembered that they were Christians,
PETER:	And eating an Indian's heart doesn't really sound like something Christ would do.
PHIL P:	The Indian didn't say anything, because,
PETER:	of course,
PHIL P:	he was dead.
PHIL A:	Good heavens!
PETER:	exclaimed the chief of the Indians,
PHIL A:	These people aren't friendly.
DAVID:	Depends on what you man by friendly,
PETER:	said the medicine man.
PHIL A:	Depends on what you mean by people,
PHIL P:	said the chief. And he shot an arrow at the soldier, which bounced off the soldier's armor.

PETER:	Nyah, nyah, nyah!
DAVID:	said the minister's wife, raising her buckly musket.
PHIL P:	Bang!
PHIL A:	said the musket.
PETER:	And a couple more Indians fell dead, clutching their intestines
PHIL P:	which spilled out on the ground.
PETER:	Well, folks, that pretty much got things going and there was a good deal of shooting and dodging behind trees and skulking and so on.
PHIL P:	The Indians killed a few settlers.
DAVID:	And the settlers killed lots of Indians.
PHIL A:	And the feast was still untouched.
PHIL P:	And it looked as if America was to be made safe for democracy —
PETER:	when!
PHIL A:	All of a sudden a very strange and unprecedented thing happened.
PETER:	What happened was,
PHIL A:	all the White people turned into Black people.
PETER & PHIL P:	Zap!
DAVID:	Like that.
PHIL A:	All the White people turned into Black people.
PHIL P:	Now you may think this amazed and befuddled the Indians.

DAVID:	Not so!
PETER:	The Indians all turned into Chinese.
PETER & PHIL P:	Bonggg!
PHIL A:	This was quite a turn of events!
PHIL P:	I'm black all over,
DAVID:	said Goody Proctor.
PHIL A:	So they burned her as a witch.
PHIL P:	Oooooo!
PETER:	We felt bad about it thereafter,
PHIL P:	when we realized we was all Black too.
PETER:	Over on the other side of the table
PHIL P:	things weren't exactly crystal clear either.
PHIL A:	I'm Yellow all over,
PHIL P:	cried the chief.
PETER:	Well, folks, a funny thing happened.
DAVID:	The settlers took off their buckles and started dancing and decorating themselves,
PHIL P:	and the Indians contemplated a lot,
DAVID:	and a few days later, someone
PHIL A:	I think it was the minister,
DAVID:	said,
PETER:	What about that war we was having?

PHIL P:	Hear, hear!
PHIL A:	said the rest of the Blacks.
PHIL P:	What were we fighting about?
PETER:	We was going to take their land,
DAVID:	said someone.
PHIL P:	Unthinkable!
PHIL A:	said the Blacks.
PETER:	And besides,
DAVID:	said someone else,
PETER:	What do you mean, "their land?"
PHIL A:	Yes, you see, having taken off their buckles and turned Black, they understood the principle of guardianship,
PHIL P:	as opposed to ownership,
PETER:	of the land.
DAVID:	After a while the Black people and the Yellow people met socially,
PETER:	and some hanky-panky took place among the younger folk,
PHIL A:	and everything got sort of blended together.
PETER:	And one day, they all looked around and there was
PHIL P:	nothing
DAVID:	but
PHIL A:	Indians! That's right, folks!

DAVID:	Nothing
PHIL P:	but
PETER:	Indians!
PHIL P:	You see,
PHIL A:	(here comes the punchline)
PETER:	the definition of an Indian is:
DAVID:	A White man
PHIL P:	who becomes a Black man
PHIL A:	with some Yellow added in.
PETER:	Some may say that's an over-simplification.
DAVID:	That's an over-simplification!
PHIL P:	But it's better than killing people.
PHIL A:	Isn't it?

BLACKOUT

THE FUSE OF DOOM!
A Hortebagy International Production
EPISODES 1 and 7

Written by The Firesign Theatre for their second run
at the Ash Grove in June, 1968.
This piece provided half the cast of
"The Giant Rat of Sumatra," Firesign's 1973 LP.

ORIGINAL CAST
Phil Austin as Charles Foster Dudley, Boris

Peter Bergman as Jonas Acme,
Andrew "The Pig" Lungit

David Ossman as the Professors Arktype

Phil Proctor as Benway, Jim Fang, Frank Acme
And "Mr. X" as The Electrician

THE FUSE OF DOOM!
Episode One

ELECTRONIC MUSIC THEME IN AND UNDER

VOICE OVER: Hortebagy Internatonal Pictures Presents: "The Fuse of Doom!" A new Frank Acme Serial Thriller, starring Andrew T. P. Lungit as Millionaire Industrialist Jonas Acme, Marshal Camp as his son and ward, Frank Acme, P. ("Wee") Rodriguez as Newspaper Magnate Charles Foster Dudley, and Rex Spofford as Professor Immanuel Arktype, O.D. With "Mr. X" as The Electrician. And now, Chapter One: "Should Old Aquaintance Be Forgot?"

THE THEME SEGUES TO HOT JAZZ, CIRCA 1920.

THE SCENE: ACME'S LIBRARY. ARKTYPE, ACME AND DUDLEY, WITH CIGARS AND CHAMPAGNE GLASSES. THE BUTLER, BENWAY, ENTERS AND POURS OUT CHAMPAGNE. HE TAKES A SWIG OUT OF THE BOTTLE HIMSELF. HE WHISPERS IN ACME'S EAR.

ACME: Are you quite sure, Benway?

BENWAY: Not at all, sir.

ACME: Thank you.

BENWAY: You're welcome.

ACME: You may go, Benway.

BENWAY DOES NOT LEAVE. ACME LOOKS AT HIS WATCH.

ACME: Gentlemen, the time has come. Both of Mickey's hands are pointing to 12 at last. Welcome to 1920!

EVERYONE SINGS "SHOULD OLD AQUAINTANCE BE FORGOT..."

ACME: Gentlemen, before we toast in the new decade, you are no doubt wondering what strange reasons compelled me to draw you away from the mammoth celebration in the Grand Ballroom of the east wing.

DUDLEY: I've never seen a happier mammoth . . .

ARKTYPE: I'll drink to that.

ACME: Not yet, Professor.

DUDLEY: Then explain yourself, Acme. Is this one of your blasted practical jokes?

ARKTYPE: Jonas, I think we've kept Mr. Dudley in suspense long enough.

ACME: Exactly, Professor. Keeping a story of this magnitude from an old cub reporter like Charles Foster Dudley has been no easy task. But that's exactly what we intend to do.

DUDLEY: The information which we are about to reveal must not go beyond the walls of this room.

ACME: Benway . . .

BENWAY: Yes, sir.

ACME: Draw the curtains as you leave.

BENWAY: Yes, sir.

BENWAY PROCEEDS TO DRAW THE CURTAINS ON A LARGE PAD OF PAPER.

DUDLEY: I don't know what you're up to, Acme. But I can tell you right now, that if what you say is of any consequence to the little people . . .

ARKTYPE: You mean the leprechauns?

DUDLEY: No! The working man! Then it is my sworn duty as publisher of the Dudley News, The Dudley Star, The Dudley Planet and the Saturday Evening Dudley to make known all the facts.

ACME: Would your sentiments remain unchanged if the man directly responsible for the incredible discovery you are about to see is none other than the legendary Dr. Immanuel Arktype.

DUDLEY: Arktype? I thought he was dead.

ARKTYPE: I am.

DUDLEY: But you went down on the Lusitania.

ARKTYPE: When the Lusitania went down, it went down without me.

DUDLEY: But — why?

ARKTYPE: I wasn't on the Lusitania.

DUDLEY: What were you on?

ARKTYPE: Opium.

DUDLEY: I thought you were on sabbatical.

ARKTYPE: That too. Whoopee! What a weekend that was! But I used the time wisely — perfecting a device which has for years deluded the greatest minds of science.

ACME: Yes. And I am turning over my entire industrial resources to investigate the potentialities of this, the most miraculous scientific achievement of this already miraculous century. Doctor . . .

ARKTYPE: The Zeppelin Tube!

HE REVEALS THE TUBE.

DUDLEY: Fantastic! I see now why you pledged us to secrecy.

	If this device ever fell into the wrong hands, I shudder to think of the catatonic consequences for all mankind.
ARKTYPE:	Exactly! The Zeppelin Tube can be a great tool — for good, or for evil.
ACME:	And Dr. Arktype has entrusted that decision to me.
DUDLEY:	What a fantastic story. I only wish I could print it.
ARKTYPE:	Now, gentlemen, the toast I promised you.

BENWAY FINISHES DRAWING THE CURTAINS AND SERVES A PLATE OF TOAST. DOING SO, HE HANDS A NOTE TO DUDLEY. DUDLEY READS IT AND RISES.

DUDLEY:	Excuse me, I've just learned that I have to go to the bathroom.
ACME:	Not before the toast, surely. Benway can go for you.
DUDLEY:	Benway, could you go for me?
BENWAY:	Yes, sir, I think I could.

BENWAY GIVES DUDLEY A BIG KISS AND LEAVES.

ACME:	Gentlemen, we three have been entrusted with a great and dangerous mission — a safe and practical use for the Zeppelin Tube.

SUDDENLY, THE LIGHTS GO OUT! THE ELECTRICIAN'S EERIE THEME MUSIC IS HEARD. THE LIGHTS FLICKER AS THE ELECTRICIAN SPEAKS.

ELECTRICIAN:	Ha ha ha! We meet again, gentlemen! Thank you for bringing this extraordinary device to my attention. I have long awaited an opportunity to put it to good use. Ha ha ha!

THE FLICKERING TURNS INTO A FULL BLACKOUT. THE MUSIC CRESCENDOS AND THE LIGHTS COME ON AGAIN.

ACME:	(His voice has a bad connection) 'here are you, you 'iend?
DUDLEY:	He must be in the house! If that fiend ever finds The Zeppelin Tube . . .
ACME:	The Zeppelin Tube! It's gone!

SO IT IS, AND DR. ARKTYPE SITS STUNNED IN HIS CHAIR.

DUDLEY:	Something's happened to Dr. Arktype! Look at that glassy stare in his mouth!
ACME:	It's a fuse! A blown fuse!

A BIG MUSIC STING AS ARKTYPE FALLS TO THE FLOOR.

DUDLEY:	Let's get him in the chair.

THEY TRY TO DO SO AS FRANK ACME ENTERS.

FRANK:	I parked the plane, Dad. When are you coming back to the party? What happened to Professor Arktype?
ACME:	Frank, I don't think you've ever met my old friend and newspaper magnate, Charles Foster Dudley.
FRANK:	An honor, sir.
DUDLEY:	It's a pity we have to meet at a time like this.
ACME:	Time is of the essence, Frank. Don't ever forget that. And there's no time like this left. Dudley, we've got to get Arktype functioning again.
DUDLEY:	Frank, do you happen to have a fuse?
FRANK:	A fuse? I think I have . . . sure, here.

ONE OF THOSE MUSIC STINGS OUT OF NOWHERE.

DUDLEY:	Thank goodness! Let's see if we can't revive the poor fellow.

ACME:	It may already be too late.

DUDLEY UNSCREWS THE OLD AND SCREWS IN THE NEW FUSE. ARKTYPE BEGINS TO REVIVE, HE MUMBLES.

ACME:	He's coming around. Professor? The man who took The Zeppelin Tube — who is he? What does he want?
ARKTYPE:	Mmmmmmmmmmmmmm!
FRANK:	Sir, excuse me, but he can't talk with that fuse in his mouth.
ACME:	Good thinking, son.
DUDLEY:	I'll do it. Now then, Professor, tell us quickly — who did this to you?
ARKTYPE:	It was mmmmmmmmmmmmm
FRANK:	He's out of juice, dad.
DUDLEY:	I'll put the fuse back in.
ARKTYPE:	Rrrmmmmmmmmmmmmmm!
ACME:	Take it easy, Doctor. Don't over-excite yourself. You've had a terrible shock. Frank, keep an eye on him.
FRANK:	Yes, sir.

FRANK DOES SO, EYEING ARKTYPE AS HE BEGINS TO COME TO AND GETS UP.

DUDLEY:	Acme, I'm going to call my old friend Inspector Fang of Oriental Intelligence.
ACME:	What are you going to call him?
DUDLEY:	Jim.
ACME:	No, you mustn't!

DUDLEY: Why not?

ACME: The bottom would crumble into the marketplace of Europe and the Continent.

DUDLEY: I never thought of it that way, Acme.

ACME: Neither did I.

DUDLEY: But you're right, of course.

ARKTYPE LEAVES THE ROOM, FOLLOWED BY FRANK. DUDLEY AND ACME ARE OBLIVIOUS TO THEIR EXIT.

ACME: We must act surreptitious, but with the utmost secrecy.

DUDLEY: And there's not a moment to lose!

ACME: Let's discuss our plans over a quick jeroboam of champagne. Whoever this fiend is, we'll soon have him in our clutches.

DUDLEY: I'll drink to that!

HE LIFTS HIS GLASS HIGH, ONLY TO HAVE IT BREAK AGAINST THE CEILING.

DUDLEY: Why, what a charming ceiling. I never noticed that fresco before.

ACME: Yes, it's an original Fettucini. I had it cut off the ceiling of the men's room at the Palazzo del' Lozzi in Paparazzi, just outside of Amsterdam.

DUDLEY: How far outside Amsterdam?

ACME: About two thousand miles.

THE CEILING IS COMING DOWN, FORCING THE MEN TO BEND AND FINALLY LIE ON THEIR BACKS.

DUDLEY: I should have recognized the Fettucini perspective. You feel as though your nose is right inside the central figure of the tableau. Who is she?

ACME: That's the Mona Lozzi.

DUDLEY: His painstaking concern for minute detail is truly impressive.

ACME: Quite. Overpowing.

DUDLEY: My god! The ceiling is moving down on us!

ACME: No, it's the floor, moving up!

DUDLEY: Help! Help!

ACME: It's no use! We're doomed!

ANOTHER BIG MUSIC STING, FOLLOWED BY THE ELECTRICIAN'S THEME. THE LIGHTS FLICKER AS HE SPEAKS.

ELECTRICIAN: The Electrician strikes again! Ha ha ha!

VOICEOVER: Be sure and be at this theatre next week for "The Curse of Cobra Valley" — Chapter Two of "The Fuse of Doom!"

MUSIC UP AND OUT WITH A BLACKOUT

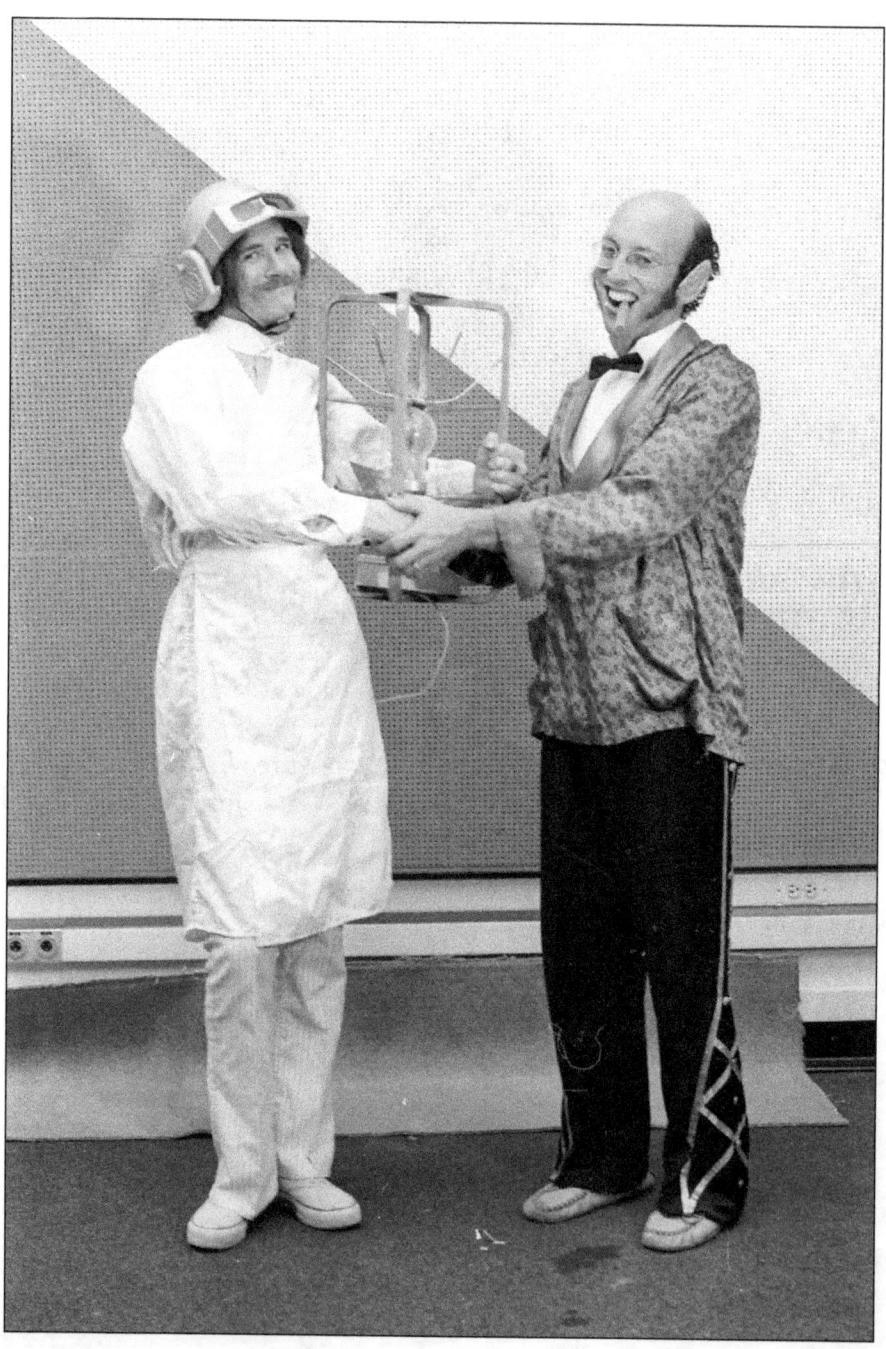

THE FUSE OF DOOM, PART SEVEN

ELECTRONIC MUSIC IN AND UNDER.

VOICEOVER: Hortebagy International Pictures presents: "The Fuse of Doom" — a new Frank Acme Serial Thriller, starring Marshall Camp as Andrew "The Pig" Lungitt, Rex Spoffard as P. ("Wee") Rodriguez, Vivian Della Chiesa as Vim Kunsthundt, and Abe Lastfogle as The Asiatic Detective. With "Mr. X" as The Electrician.

ELECTRONIC MUSIC CROSSFADES TO AN ORIENTAL THEME.

VOICEOVER: As you remember in Chapter Six, after escaping from the Cobramen, Frank Acme set about once again in his relentless pursuit of the missing Zeppelin Tube and its radio-controlled inventor, Dr. Immanuel Arktype. Meanwhile, Frank's friend and fellow crime-buster, Jim Fang, The Asiatic Detective, armed only with his arms and his intimate knowledge of Karate, Sume and Watanabe, was ambushed by one of The Electrician's henchmen, deadly Andrew "The Pig" Lungit, who kills only with his powerful hands. And now, Chapter Seven — "Care of the Cow Brings Good Fortune."

IN THE NEXT WORDLESS SCENE, JIM FANG AND ANDREW CONFRONT EACH OTHER. FANG DOES ELABORATE KARATE BUSINESS. LUNGIT SHOOTS FANG WITH HIS FINGER. FANG DROPS LIKE A STONE. BLACKOUT.

A MUSICAL SUSPENSE BRIDGE.

THE NEXT SCENE IS IN THE ELECTRICIAN'S LAIR. DR. CARBON ARKTYPE, TWIN BROTHER TO EMMANUEL, IS SETTING UP EQUIPMENT, WHILE BORIS READS NEWS ITEMS OFF A CLIPBOARD.

BORIS: Moon's in Gemini. Earthquake in Japan.

HE STICKS A PUSHPIN INTO A MAP.

DR. CARBON: Splendid. Tremors in the Aleutians. Jupiter's in the North Node.

BORIS: Schoolbus collision in Fort Wayne. Farmer coughs up towel in Brussels.

DR. CARBON: Neptune 31 degrees 4 minutes retrograde in Scorpio. I'm glad we did that.

BORIS: Did we?

DR. CARBON: And that's nothing compared to what havoc we can wreak once I learn what to do with the Infernal Zeppelin Tube.

A SUDDEN BEEP-BEEP-BEEP ON THE RADIO SET.

DR. CARBON: Good heavens! What time is it?

BORIS: It's lunchtime.

DR. CARBON: Then it must be The Pig's report from the concrete submarine. I'll see if I can get a fix on him. Red Death, calling The Pig.

BORIS: Are you getting anything?

DR. CARBON: Well, now and again on the side. Quiet! Something's coming through.

HE PUTS ON A PAIR OF ANTIQUE EARPHONES.

BORIS: What is it, Doctor?

DR. CARBON: Paul Whiteman. Would you care to dance?

BORIS: Can you hear anything?

DR. CARBON: What?

BORIS:	Can you hear anything?
DR. CARBON:	Not with these damned earphones on! Wait! He's coming through. Boris, give him The Electrician's message.
BORIS:	Hello, Andy? What's new? You killed Jim Fang. Who's he? A friend of yours. That's wonderful, Andy. How was the rest of your vacation?
DR. CARBON:	The message, you fool!
BORIS:	Right. Andy? Pick up Joe From Chicago in the concrete submarine . . .
DR. CARBON:	Use the code!
BORIS:	Oh. Hello, Mother? Pick up the overshoes in the linen closet. What? I'm sorry I left them there. Yes, I'll clean up my room. Yes, Mother, yes. What? Of course I love you. I tried to call you on Sunday, but I was busy. But, Mother, that's silly. Please don't cry. Alright, Mother, here. (Give her a big kiss over the mike.) Now, Mom, listen carefully to this. Pick up the overshoes in the linen closet and bring them home. Use the secret knock. I'm signing off now. O-F-F. Goodbye, Andrew.

THE ELECTRICIAN'S THEME MUSIC. LIGHTS FLICKERING. THE ELECTRICIAN APPEARS IN COSTUME.

ELECTRICIAN:	Hello, men. What's happening?
BORIS:	We just got today's results, Master. If you look at the map there, you'll see a little teeny dot there. What does that mean, Doc?
DR. CARBON:	It means firestorm in Shanghai, owing to the sudden conjunction of Mars and the Crabs.
ELECTRICIAN:	Who is responsible for this?
BORIS:	He is.
DR. CARBON:	He is.

ELECTRICIAN: Wonderful. You're both to be condemned. But not now.

BORIS: Master, Fang is dead.

ELECTRICIAN: Splendid! Who is Master Fang?

BORIS: A friend of Andrew's.

ELECTRICIAN: Splendid! Who is Andrew?

BORIS: Your deadly henchman. He's bringing Joe From Chicago here any minute.

ELECTRICIAN: Wonderful, wonderful! The world will soon be over the brink of chaos, and we will be responsible for it, and all because of the Zeppelin Tube. Ha ha ha. I'm going to the bathroom.

THE ELECTRICIAN STRIDES OUT.

DR. CARBON: But the Zeppelin . . . damn! Couldn't get his attention.

BORIS: He's a busy man. In and out of his secret bathroom hideout all day.

DR. CARBON: He must loosen his fanatic hold over the Zeppelin Tube. My machine is all ready for it. The Tube alone is worthless without the telecommunicator and the ever-ready Death Ray.

BORIS: And they are useless without the . . .

DR CARBON: Zeppelin Tube.

BORIS: Zeppelin Tube.

DR. CARBON: Correct.

BORIS: Thank god.

A KNOCKING AT THE DOOR.

BORIS:	Is that the secret knock?
DR. CARBON:	I don't know. It's a secret.
BORIS:	I don't recognize it either.
DR. CARBON:	That's it then. Let him in.

ANDREW LUNGIT ENTERS. BEHIND HIM IS "JOE" — ACTUALLY FRANK ACME.

BORIS:	Hi, Andy.
LUNGIT:	Hi, fellas. I should like for you to meet a very dangerous criminal and a hell of a nice guy — Joe From Chicago.
BORIS:	Oh, yeah?
FRANK:	Yeah.
BORIS:	Where's the Chicago Water Tower?
FRANK:	Right where I left it.
BORIS:	Where?
FRANK:	Chicago.
BORIS:	I guess he's okay, Andrew. Well, you're just in time for lunch. Come away from your infernal Death Ray and eat. Joe From Chicago, this is our scientific genius, Doc Arktype.

AN OMINOUS MUSIC STING.

FRANK:	How do you do, Doc. (Sotto) I'll have you out of here in an hour, sir.
DR. CARBON:	What?
FRANK:	Sshhhh!
BORIS:	Come over here and eat, Joe From Chicago.

FRANK:	No, thank you. I brought my own lunch.
LUNGIT:	Wonderful. We ain't got enough to go around anyway. Here, Doc, have a piece of pie.

FRANK CONSTRUCTS A TRANSMITTER FROM HIS LUNCH ITEMS. THE OTHERS TRY TO EAT SQUEAKY PLASTIC DOG TOYS THAT LOOK LIKE FOOD. FRANK USES A PICKLE AS A MICROPHONE AND A BREADSTICK AS AN ANTENNA.

FRANK:	Hello, Dad? This is Frank. Dad, I can hardly hear you. Wait a minute, I'll adjust the antenna. Ah! That's much better. Dad, I found Dr. Arktype and he's . . . and he's with you. No, he's with me. I know that's what you said. But there can't be two Dr. Arktypes. Oh, there can? His twin what?

AS LUNGIT RISES AND APPROACHES HIM, FRANK BITES THE TOP OFF THE BREADSTICK.

FRANK:	Mmmm, good! Nothing like the smell of fresh bread.
LUNGIT:	'Scuse me, Joe From Chicago. I gotta take a leak.

HE EXITS AND AS HE DOES, HE TALKS BACK OVER HIS SHOULDER.

LUNGIT:	Oh, by the way, as soon as you've finished lunch, The Electrician wants to talk to you.
FRANK:	You mean — The Electrician? Right here in the same room? Me and him together? I gotta take a leak too!

FRANK RUSHES OUT.

DR. CARBON:	That was a wonderful lunch!
BORIS:	I don't know about that Joe From Chicago.
LUNGIT:	What do you mean?
BORIS:	I don't know what I mean. But I just hope the Master knows what he's doing, bringing in outside help.

LUNGIT: The Boss always knows what he's doing. Otherwise he wouldn't be called The Electrician.

THE LIGHTS FLICKER AS THE ELECTRICIAN'S THEME IS HEARD AGAIN. THE ELECTRICIAN ENTERS.

ELECTRICIAN: Hello, men, what's happening?

LUNGIT: Joe From Chicago is here, Boss.

ELECTRICIAN: Joe From Chicago? I don't know any Joe From Chicago.

BORIS: What? But, Master . . .

ELECTRICIAN: Quiet! Bring him before me. I want to see him.

BORIS: You mean right here in the same room? You and him together? Now?

ELECTRICIAN: Right now! And I'm going to the bathroom!

HE RUNS OUT.

BORIS: I told you so.

LUNGIT: All right, all right! Let's go get him.

FRANK RUNS IN.

FRANK: Hiya, fellas! Now that's what I call a bathroom!

LUNGIT: You're not Joe From Chicago!

FRANK: I'm not? Just a second, I'll go get him.

FRANK RUNS OUT AGAIN.

BORIS: You see, the Master was right.

ONCE AGAIN, THE FLICKERING LIGHTS AND ELECTRICIAN'S THEME. THE ELECTRICIAN ENTERS.

ELECTRICIAN:	Who's that in my bathroom?
LUNGIT:	It's not Joe From Chicago.
DR. CARBON:	Only one man could be brave and resourceful enough to penetrate to this secret underground lair — Frank Acme!
ELECTRICIAN:	Well, whoever he is, he's in my bathroom. How can I get any reading done? Boys, if we don't capture this young scamp immediately or sooner, all our plans will go down the drain. Which reminds me. I'm going to the bathroom! Follow me!

THE ELECTRICIAN AND LUNGIT RACE OUT, LEAVING DR. CARBON AND ARKTYPE ALONE FOR A MOMENT. THEN FRANK ENTERS.

FRANK:	Pssssst, professor! I've got the Tube! We can make a break for it.
DR. CARBON:	Don't break it, you fool! Give it to me! While you're at it, give it to him!

THIS DIRECTION TO LUNGIT, WHO ENTERS BEHIND FRANK. LUNGIT SOCKS FRANK.

DR. CARBON:	Meddling fool. Tie him to that chair while I make my final adjustments on The Zeppelin Tube. Frank Acme will be our first victim. Evil, evil, evil . . .
FRANK:	(coming to) Where am I? Who am I?
LUNGIT:	Joe From Chicago?
FRANK:	Stop that! I'm young Frank Acme. That's Dr. Immanuel Arktype and he ought to be ashamed of himself!
DR. CARBON:	I'm Dr. Carbon Arktype, twin brother to that fool Immanuel, and I'm certainly not ashamed of myself. Evil, evil, evil . . .
FRANK:	We feared that The Electrician, in his despicable madness, would use the Zeppelin Tube to further his

The Fuse of Doom!, Part Seven

own diabolical designs — but to see you, an American scientist, aiding and abetting this fiendish crime, motivated only by jealousy of your ingenious, saintly brother . . . Well, I've never been so pissed off in all my life!

DR. CARBON: Silence, you fool!

LUNGIT STUFFS A GAG IN FRANK'S MOUTH.

DR. CARBON: The Death Ray capacitor is fully charged, and we're ready to activate the Ray itself. Andrew, turn off the lights. We need all the power we can get!

THERE IS A BLACKOUT AND THE ELECTRICIAN'S THEME PLAYS.

ELECTRICIAN: Ha ha ha. This will teach you, you impertinent upstart, that meddling with The Electrician will lead to nasty consequences. After we're through with you, my master plan will be put into operation, and the first place to feel the awesome power of The Zeppelin Ray will be The Windy City — New York! Ha ha ha ha and I just went to the bathroom!

THE MOVIE SERIAL THEME SEGUES IN.

VOICEOVER: Be sure and be at this theatre next week for "Lighting Strikes Twice" — Chapter Eight of "The Fuse of Doom!"

THEME FADES OUT.

THE COUNT OF MONTE CRISTO

Written by The Firesign Theatre for their second run at the Ash Grove in June, 1968 and continually revised between then and their fourth appearance in November, 1970. It was part of their repertoire for their first East Coast Tour in April, 1970.

More scenes were added for "The Martian Space Party" in 1972 and a full-length version was created in 1980, when it was titled "Anythynge You Want To — Shakespeare's Lost Comedie."

It has been in their repertoire for over 40 years.

ORIGINAL CAST

Phil Austin as Andrew Lunch, Edmund Edmund

Peter Bergman as Nuncle Bishop

David Ossman as Prologue, Duke

Phil Proctor as Edmund

THE COUNT OF MONTE CRISTO

PROLOG: Admit me Prologue to this Dreadful Piece,
While on your arses, warming up the seats,
And find no cause to leave, for doors
Are barred behind thine unsuspecting feets.
So suffer us to succor you, al fresco,
With this our play, "The Mount of County Crisco."
But! Lo and Hi! Here comes good master Peter,
Say! He'll cry out "Uncle, uncle" at the last,
But at the first our Nuncle he'll portray —
A vile man, and in his vial he keeps a viper hid
To do in Edmond Dantes, the Orphan Count —
He's no Count's kid — count the Counts
As we proceed — it's no account to me . . .
Who's he? 'Tis him! No, no, it's not! But
How his darksome mien and mean demeanor mean
But we know not — 'tis the sickness of the age.
I'll play the Ancient Duke — and leave the stage.

BOOM BOOM OF WIND AND DRUMS

GHOST: Hellooooooo . . . !

GUARD: Who's there? Stand and expose yourself.

GHOST: Long live the King!

GUARD: Bernardo?

GHOST: He.

GUARD: (ASIDE) Tis King Bernardo.

GHOST:	Sleep sits moistly 'pon my face this clammy night. What be thy name, my trusty friend? Go, rusty clod, now wend thy way to bed. While you relieve yourself upon yon wall, I'll relieve thee of thy watch . . .

THE GHOST DOES SO AND VANISHES. THE GUARD PEES.

GUARD:	That Ghost! He took my watch! Tis yet another portent I have seen upon this portholed wall, whereon I write my name. And dot the "I" for Infamy, that circumsized both Count and Court like a passing plane.
2ND GUARD:	Hola!
GUARD:	Who's there?
2ND GUARD:	'Tis I, Andrew Lunch, your battle-mate. Put up your pike — the pigs have supped.
GUARD:	Then let's pick up our pikes and strike a pose as prelude to their entrance.

ENTER THE DUKE AND FRIAR BEEPO

DUKE:	What a wonderful supper! But, alas, Friar Beepo — my final hour draws neigh, and still no word from that bastard, Edmond!
BEEPO:	Marster, marster! Don't exert yerself needlessly, yer Lordship, over that bastard, yer worthless nephew.
DUKE:	Gazundheit!

ENTER THE BISHOP NUNCLE

NUNCLE:	How liked you the piece of poisoned cod, brother? Twas of mine own making.
DUKE:	I liked it passing well, and so I passed it by. It bore your stamp.

NUNCLE: (ASIDE) The bore, he would not lick my cancelled stamp, post haste! A cancelling stamp I mean. And yet — I know not what I mean!!

THE DUKE SITS

DUKE: And so good brother Bishop — here we sit.

THEY COMPETE FOR THE ONE CHAIR

DUKE: Not you, but We — who've stuffed our gullets to the stuffing point and signed the treaty with the cows. Our virgin niece is padlocked for the Spanish Prince. Faire Normandie is ours.

NUNCLE: Faire Normandie is ours! (ASIDE) S'blood I care! For how am I to turn a dandy leg at court, unless a dandy legacy is turned to me, from him, I mean. And yet I speak so fast I know not what I mean.

DUKE: Nor I. Nor all us here. But, alas, hairless brother . . . my final hour draws nigh — and still no word from that bastard Edmond.

NUNCLE: Your worthless nephew? Would you give an airing to, and make an heir of one who puts on airs and gives you nothing, brother mine, but air?! He errs, by Gemini! An errant air-sign and a Jew!

DUKE: A Jew?

NUNCLE: A Jew.

DUKE: Goodbye, begone, Adieu.

NUNCLE: But what dost meanst by that?

DUKE: Split!

NUNCLE: Then they'll be two of me!

NUNCLE LEAVES

DUKE: I like him better not at all.

AFTER AN OFF-STAGE DISTURBANCE, EDMOND ENTERS

EDMOND: Your niece, my cousin, refused to bar me entrance to your rooms, Nuncle. Is it true that you are ailing? Well, so am I!

DUKE: We'll speak of that anon, my boy . . .

EDMOND: And on and on and on . . . 'Til then, farewell. I'll see you soon in Hell.

DUKE: Wait! Before I am to slip into that silly sleep of sleeps, I needs must reveal to you a great and awful secret . . .

EDMOND: (YAWNING) Oh, Nuncle, Nuncle — speak not of sleeping . . .

DUKE: Come my beaming basket boy! Come, bend over! You, Edmond Dantes, are not an orphan foundling as you think, but the only son and true and rightful heir to the weighty fortunes of the Count of . . . aaaaaghhh!

THE COUNT DIES

EDMOND: I don't know any Count of Aaaaaghh! I know a Duke of Rgggh!

BEEPO: Oh, piteous time! The bastard's dead! I'll bear these tidings to the Queen — in bed!

BEEPO LEAVES

EDMOND: Oh, mercenary destiny, that marbles up the sweetened tooth of time with black disguise. I'll fill my bucket silly with revenge, 'til blood shall douche the anger from mine eyes.

THE NUNCLE BISHOP ENTERS

NUNCLE: Nephew!

EDMOND:	Gazundheit!
NUNCLE:	Your couplet runneth over. But, come — in this our hour of mutual greed, we'll share a flagon of churning burgundy — Nippon Cadet '62. (ASIDE) And now my action's clear — and now I'll do't! This foundling cur was known to be my brother's favorite and thus is bound to find some favor in his will. And so, to flavor my good fortunes, I'll pack him off to Heaven by this poison draft, to be my brother's keeper, and thus to keep the better's best myself! (TO EDMOND) Here's drink for you!
EDMOND:	Sweet Uncle! Here's drink for you!

THEY TOAST, JOIN ARMS AND TOAST AGAIN AND DRINK (FROM THEIR OWN GOBLETS)

NUNCLE:	It won't be long. E'en now the venom surges to his brain — Death's knocking at his door and yet he smiles — He'll drop like a stone . . .

NUNCLE DIES

EDMOND:	He's no fun, he fell right over. What? Dead drunk! Nay, dead again! Where is his smiles, his curdling mirth? They've left me groatless, to seek the secret of my secret birth! I'll take some speed and beat the Queen to Perth!

"MARIE" ENTERS

MARIE:	Oh, no, you don't!
EDMOND:	Ah, my fiancée, Cousine Marie! A kiss for thee?
MARIE:	No, no! Oui, oui! I'm not your fiancée!
EDMOND:	What say you, greasy wrench?

HALFWAY THROUGH THE FOLLOWING LINE, "MARIE" RIPS OFF HER DRAG AND HER VOICE DROPS AN OCTAVE.

MARIE:	Unbeknownst to you, I am your twin brother, Edmond, Edmond!

MARIE MIMES A GIANT PHALLUS, WHICH SHE THEN SWINGS OVER HER SHOULDER

EDMOND:	Edmond Edmond? Is't true? Then we can never be married!
MARIE:	And you shall never live to inherit my father's fortunes!
EDMOND:	Why should I take a woman's word for that?
MARIE:	Enough said! En garde, you swine!
EDMOND:	I'll guard my swine 'til death do part us both! Have at you!
MARIE:	Gazundheit!

THEY FIGHT WITH THE SWORDS OF INVISIBILITY. "CLANG! CLANG! CLANG!" BACK AND FORTH. EDMOND DISARMS MARIE. "HER" SWORD FLIES UP AND WHEN IT FALLS "SHE" CATCHES IT IN HER THROAT. MARIE DIES DRAMATICALLY.

EDMOND:	She's dead and gone and still she acts! Beautiful, even in death.

THE DUKE, SITTING "DEAD" IN HIS CHAIR ALL THIS TIME, COMES TO LIFE.

DUKE:	Well fought, my son!
EDMOND:	My Nuncle's ghost!
DUKE:	Not your Nuncle, but your Dad!
EDMOND:	My Father's ghost?
DUKE:	Not a ghost neither!
EDMOND:	Not — my Father?

DUKE:	Yes, my son!
EDMOND:	Then — I — am your son?
DUKE:	No! I'm your father! And I have proof! Read what is writ upon your dagger's dirk, the twin to mine.
EDMOND:	This plastic dagger, given me at birth?
DUKE:	The very same.
EDMOND:	"I am he of whom he speaks." That's proof enough for me.

NUNCLE BISHOP, THOUGHT DEAD, REMARKS:

NUNCLE:	And me!

MARIE RISES FROM THE DEAD:

MARIE:	Me too.
DUKE:	We are agreed! And so we seal our secret kinship with a kiss.
EDMOND:	Son!
DUKE:	Father!

RUNNING TO EMBRACE ONE ANOTHER, EACH FALLS UPON THE PLASIC DAGGER HELD BY THE OTHER.

DUKE:	Alas! I'm hurt!
EDMOND:	Me too!
NUNCLE & MARIE:	And so are we all, all us here!
DUKE:	I die, I die, alas! There's nothing more to say . . .
EDMOND:	And no one left to write an ending to this dumb-ass play.

THEY BOW AND DIE. ALL BOW AND DIE AGAIN.

CURTAIN, IF ANY

Ash Grove 'Blues Bash'

You are cordially invited to the

Ash Grove 'Blues Bash'

featuring

CANNED HEAT

plus BIG JOE WILLIAMS

Dec. 15-18

TAJ MAHAL

AND GROUP !!!

Dec. 19-21

LIGHTNIN' HOPKINS

PLUS

FIRESIGN THEATER

Dec. 25 - Jan. 4

RSVP 653-2070

"...ND OF THE WORLD"

A piece written as a TV script in July, 1968. It gave birth to "End of Son . . . " in 1969 and to "Lawyer's Hospital," "Over The Edge" and "Who's Peggy?" — later Firesign soap-operas.

ORIGINAL CAST
Phil Austin as Carstairs

Peter Bergman as Ned

David Ossman as Announcer, Aubrey

Phil Proctor as the Intern

"...ND OF THE WORLD"

ORGAN THEME UP. FADE UP ON PROGRAM LOGO (CITY SILHOUETTED, WITH KING KONG ON THE EMPIRE STATE OR SOMETHING LIKE IT).

ANNOUNCER: ...d of the World" — the continuing story of love and human compassion in a small town that understands neither, but rejects both. Brought to you this week and every week.

ORGAN CUE: DRAMATIC TRANSITION

FADE UP ON CU OF URINE SPECIMEN CARRIED BY INTERN WHO WALKS DOWN HOSPITAL CORRIDOR.

SOUND: Hospital Intercom and bells.
"There will be a sale of personal effects in the 3rd floor waiting room." "Will Dr. John the Night-Tripper please report to makeup." "Dr. John to makeup." "Dr. Roberts, Dr. Roberts, report to Dr. Filth in the Emergency Ward. Imperative." Etc.

CAMERA SETTLES ON MED SHOT OF DOOR LABLED MENSROOM? DOOR OPENS TO REVEAL DR. CARSTAIRS SR. IN FULL SURGICAL GARB. HE IS EXHAUSTED? AND PREOCCUPIED, AS HE TAKES OFF MASK AND UNDOES HIS GOWN.

INTERN (OC): Doctor? Doctor?

CARSTAIRS: (groggily) What is it?

INTERN: Dr. Carstairs, I've got to talk to you.

CARSTAIRS: I'm not Dr. Carstairs, my boy.

INTERN: I've got to talk to someone, Dad.

CARSTAIRS: Well, then, what is it (Looking at name tag) Dr. Carstairs?

INTERN: I'm having trouble identifying Mrs. Wilson's stomach and . . .

CARSTAIRS: Perhaps if you spent less time in obstetrics with Nurse Warren and more time with your Probation Officer . . . well, do you remember what we talked about at the lake last summer?

INTERN: Gee, Dad — I told you I was sorry then and I'm still sorry now.

CARSTAIRS: (pause) Does Peggy know that?

DR. EXITS DOWN THE HALL, LEAVING INTERN IN AN AGONIZED CU.

ORGAN — DRAMATIC TRANSITION.

SEGUE TO PHONE RINGING. WE ARE IN THE CARSTAIRS' LIVING ROOM WHERE UNCLE NED IS WATCHING HIMSELF ON TV.

NED: Marge? Get the phone, will you? Marge? Peggy? Phoebe? Jocelyn? Heidi? Stephanie? Yslsdid? Oh, those dwarfs are never around when you need 'em.

HE ANSWERS THE PHONE.

NED: Hello . . .

SOUND CUE — DOOR CHIMES.

NED: . . . Just a minute, there's someone at the door.

HE LAYS THE PHONE DOWN AND CROSSES TO DOOR AND OPENS IT.

NED: Aubrey. What are you doing here? Didn't Dr. Carstairs tell you to keep away from his wife?

AUBREY:	(entering room) Watch your blood pressure, Uncle Ned. I'm not here to see Peggy. I'm here to see you.
NED:	Why?
AUBREY:	I don't know, but I'll (pause) think of something.

AUBREY CROSSES TO THE BAR, POURS HIMSELF A STIFF ONE, HUMMING SOFTLY.

AUBREY:	Love me tender, love me true . . .
NED:	Just what do you want from me, Aubrey?
AUBREY:	A little (pause) drink. What about you, Uncle Ned?
NED:	Stop tormenting me. You know I haven't touched a drop since the fire.
AUBREY:	That was this morning. Are you going to let it haunt you the rest of your life?
NED:	Why, you young punk . . . Don't forget whom you're talking to. As Editor I can have you run out of town in the next episode.
AUBREY:	Don't push your luck, Pops. Unless (pause) you'd like to print this on your front page.

AUBREY PULLS A PHOTOGRAPH FROM HIS POCKET. NED GRABS IT.

NED:	Where did you get this?
AUBREY:	Wouldn't you (pause) and Peggy like to know.
NED:	You filthy little blackmailer.

HE RIPS UP PHOTO AND HURLS IT AT AUBREY.

AUBREY:	Happy New Year to you too. (Laughs) That was my only copy.

INTERN (YOUNG DR. CARSTAIRS) HAS ENTERED ROOM UNNOTICED. HE IS CARRYING GAILY WRAPPED PACKAGES.

INTERN: Aubrey. What the devil are you doing out of jail?

REACTION SHOT OF AUBREY, SHOWING SURPRISE.

INTERN: What the devil are you doing out of jail?

REACTION SHOT OF NED, SHOWING SURPRISE.

INTERN: What the devil are you doing out of jail?

BACK TO THE MASTER SHOT.

AUBREY: Just having a friendly little (pause) drink with your Uncle Ned.

INTERN: But, Uncle Ned — you haven't touched a drop since the fire.

NED: Well, I'm not going to let that haunt me the rest of my life.

INTERN: No, Ned. I can't let you do it. Not on Peggy's birthday.

HE GRABS THE BOTTLE FROM NED. REACTION SHOTS OF NED, LOOKING HURT, INTERN, LOOKING SHOCKED, AUBREY, LOOKING UNSAVORY AND FIREMAN, WHO HAS ENTERED THE ROOM UNNOTICED.

CUT TO MASTER SHOT OF NED, INTERN AND AUBREY WATCHING THE SCENE ON THE TV SET. (REMEMBER THE TV SET?) ZOOM TO TIGHT CU OF FIREMAN.

FIREMAN: Is Peggy home?

DRAMATIC ORGAN STING.

CUT TO PHONE (REMEMBER THE PHONE?) OFF HOOK WITH FAINT VOICE ON FILTER:

FILTER VOICE: Hello? Hello? Hello? Hello?

DISSOLVE TO MAIN TITLE LOGO AND THEME IN AND UNDER.

ANNOUNCER: . . . d of the World." Another episode brought to you continuously this week and every week.

MUSIC UP AND OUT.

THE T.V. SET

Written by The Firesign Theatre and performed at various locations during Firesign's East Coast tour, March 1970.

ORIGINAL CAST

Phil Austin as Hugh Downer, Jim, Rosemary, Bob Hind, Neal, Felix Paparazzi, President Tingling, Tom Redman, Happy Hamburger, Father Groat, Drughead, Harold

Peter Bergman as Patti Pap, Mike, Bob Baseline, Dr. Math, Duck, Ed Sloat, Intern, Danny Dollar, Ida Matetsky, Admiral Groat, Joe Beets, Walter Klondike, Madge, Ed White, Dean, Andy Gerkin, Mr. Smith, Ankerman, Joey, Veronica

David Ossman as Doc the Weatherman, Kathy, Danny, Announcer Bob, Nick Gunderson, Ozzie, Catherwood, Generalissimo, Huckster, Betty, Henry Yukamoto

Phil Proctor as Professor Bob Melts, Buzz, Dr. Gunderson, Sailor Bill, Cat, Aquario, Mrs. Presky, George Matetsky, Mr. Secretary, Carl Prensky, Barbara Bobo, Rocky, Prez, Cyclamate Singer, Louise, Reverend Ferberger, Orgie, Girl, Father O'Long, Merv, Ralph Spoilsport

THE T.V. SET

SOUND:	SNORING — ALARM RINGS — ALARM OFF — YAWNS
VOICES:	Turn it off! (LIGHTING UP) Turn it on!
SOUND:	CLICK! — WHITE NOISE — TONE
ANNOUNCER:	Good morning. Station KWKW-T-TV, Indian Grave, Montana, begins its broadcast day. KWKW-T-TV is owned and operated by the Firesign Theatre Broadcasting Company, with studios and transmitters located high atop the Piute Mound. Portions of today's programming are prerecor...
HUGH:	...ood morning. I'm Hugh Downer.
PATTI:	And I'm Patti Pap.
HUGH:	And, along with Professor Bob and Doc the Weatherman, this is "Today's Day Today."
PATTI:	This is the 38th of Cunegonde, Hugh. What happened today in history?
HUGH:	Well, Patti — on this day in 1938 — B.C. — George Antrobus invented the wheel.
PATTI:	We've been on it ever since.
HUGH:	In 1889, the Peace of Humus broke out ending the 100 Year's War Against the Cows. And, last year, Patti — the world ended.

PATTI:	As we know it, Hugh.
HUGH:	You're darn tootin', Patti. Who was born today?
PATTI:	Nobody, Hugh.
HUGH:	I mean — before they changed the water, Patti.
PATTI:	Oh! Jack LaRue, George Matetsky and The Impressions.
HUGH:	It's National Groundnut Day in South Carolina; open season on bobolinks starts today in the Midwest, and I know we must have a lot of viewers back in my home state of Iowa, watching us from their trailers, guns oiled and ready.
PATTI:	Get a few for me, boys.
HUGH:	And, Professor Bob Melts — you know what else today is?
PROF:	What? Oh, yes, Hugh. It's Mortification Day. It was just a year ago that Scoutmaster Nixon was stoned in office.
PATTI:	That's why the flags are all at half-mast.
PROF:	And all the banks are open.
PATTI:	I didn't know that.
PROF:	There's a lot of things you don't know, sweetheart!
HUGH:	How's the weather, Doc?
DOC:	Well, there isn't any, Hugh — as usual. But for all those brave folks down there on the East Coast, you can look forward to one to two inches of grey snow and MIN 3 MAX 4 hours of breathing. So take it easy!

HUGH:	Thanks, doc. We'll be back in one minute with an interesting demonstration by members of the Swedish Whip Corps — opening tonight at the Winter Palace Theatre.
PATTI:	And I'll be having some back-chat with their Madame Olga, about her private impressions on American men.
HUGH:	But first, these messages...
ANNOUNCER:	The Frog returns on "Return of the Frog" tonight at 8:30.
SOUND:	COFFEE CUPS
KATHY:	Buzz? Another cup of coffee for you?
BUZZ:	Negative, honey. I've had enough.
KATHY:	How about you, Michael?
MIKE:	No, ma'am — I'll pass.
KATHY:	How about you, Jim?
JIM:	No, thanks, sugar. Ah's full up!
MUSIC:	HARP GLISSANDO
DOC:	What seems to be the matter, Kathy?
KATHY:	Well, Doctor Gunderson, I've been living with the guys for almost two months now, and everything's worked out wonderfully. Except...
DOC:	Ya?
KATHY:	They don't want it anymore, den, Dr. Gunderson.
DOC:	Don't want what den, child?
KATHY:	My coffee. They're ban tired of my coffee!

DOC:	It's ban pretty clear that your coffee don't got Zest Appeal.
KATHY:	Zest appeal? What's that?
DOC:	I don't know — because that's the Secret Ingredient in Erzatz Brothers Coffee — ya! A blend of the finest Brazilian coffee beans, Chilean chicory nuts and Spanish flies. Here — take this can home with you, Katy!
MUSIC:	HARP GLISSANDO
ANN (WHISPERS):	The next morning...
KATHY:	More coffee, boys?
JIM:	Does we want some more?!
BOYS:	Oh, lay!!
KATHY:	(SIGHS)
MUSIC:	HARP GLISSANDO
ANNOUNCER:	Erzatz Brothers Coffee — with Zest Appeal. Look for the can in the plain brown can.
MUSIC:	HARP STING
ANNOUNCER:	Cowboys battle monsters tonight at ten...
SOUND:	CLICK!
ANNOUNCER 2:	...ith the Four Bobsled Twins on "You Bet Your Half-Life" at 6:00.
BOB B:	Hi, this is Bob Baseline. Let's take a look at your car. It's screaming "Wash me please!" If you're a Mr. Common Sense, you won't believe ME when I tell YOU that I have an envelope that will clean your car while you're driving it home to work. Well, believe me, this one isn't like the Austrian

	self sharpening razor that I was offering last week. No margin of error, like in the birth control pills from Brazil. No, friends, Bob Baseline's word on it. This one won't go bad...
SOUND:	CLICK!
ANNOUNCER:	...at time is it, kids?
KIDS (OFF):	It's Gumdrop Time!
MUSIC:	KAZOO — "TEDDY BEAR'S PICNIC"
ANNOUNCER:	That's right! And here he comes now — down the marmalade gangplank of the Good Ship Gumdrop! It's loveable Sailor Bill!
BILL:	(TOOT TOOT) Hi, Gumdroppers!
KIDS:	Heil, Sailor Bill!
BILL:	Let's all drop our gum! (BURBLE TOOT TOOT) Well, who are the lucky birthday gumdroppers today? Sally Ann Chink of Sector R — 12 years old today, Sally. Little Georgie Matetsky of Old Miller's Guardhouse Road in Sector N — (I used to have an aunt who lived in Sector N, but she escaped). 3½. And Jesús Cristos, all the way from Needles. And by the way, kids — guess who else has a birthday today? Me. I'm 38.

(OFF MIKE LAUGH)

That's right, Charlie. I'm 38 years old today. And I'm standing here in a sailor suit. Yeah. Let's get to the cartoon right now. What is it? Tweetie and Sylvester... Same as yesterday — well, let's — |
| **SOUND:** | CLICK! |
| **DR. MATH:** | ...at's 2 Postmen, times 3 animal control officers, divided by 2 gas meter readers — makes how many Bendable Integrated Community Workers? Record |

	your answer — NOW. (BEEP) Did you remember to carry the Bum? Good! The answer my friends is -
SOUND:	CLICK!
ROSEMARY:	...nine oh five — and that means it's time for all us safety chiefs to go to school. Or, if you live in an Eastern time zone, to eat lunch. Now, let's all get in our prowl cars and drive to school!
KIDS:	SIRENS AND WHISTLES
ROSEMARY:	Well, here we are! And nobody seriously injured! Look — there's Disappearo the Cat, Rex the Dog and Double Duck, the schizophrenic! I do hope they're fighting today. Roll the cartoon, Jocko — and we'll all watch.
KAZOO:	FANFARE
WHISTLE:	PEER GYNT
DUCK:	Quack, quack-quack!
KAZOO:	SUSPENSE THEME
CAT:	Meeow!
DUCK:	Oh! Oh! (WHISTLES)
DOG:	BARKS
CAT AND DOG:	ANGRY CHASE
KAZOO:	WILLIAM TELL OVERTURE ENDING — DA DAAAA!
DUCK:	SAWS AND WHISTLES
KAZOO:	SUSPENSE THEME
CAT:	Meeow! Heh heh heh!

DUCK:	WHISTLES
CAT:	THREATENING MEOW
DUCK:	Oh, oh! (SAWS MADLY)
CAT:	Oh, oh! (FALLS)
SOUND:	WHISTLE AND CRASH
KAZOO:	DA! DA!
CAT:	MOANS
DUCK:	WHISTLES
CAT:	Huh? Oh, no!
SOUND:	MACHINE GUN
CAT:	DIES HORRIBLY
KAZOO:	SIGNATURE MUSIC
ANNOUNCER:	Kids! Blast off! To the wonderful world of Cartell Toys!
ANNOUNCER 2:	Aquario! The Earth Man! By day, he's Mr. Straight — a clean, dry, high-speed vibrating hygiene robot. And, he talks...
AQUARIO:	(CHUNK) Open me up and look at my seminal vesicle. (CHUNK) And this is your fallopian tube. (CHUNK) And this is my wee-wee. (CHUNK)
ANNOUNCER 3:	Then turn him on at night! Aquario's a swinger, the hard-hitting symbol of the New Age. Just listen to him rap.
AQUARIO:	(CHUNK) Hi, baby. (CHUNK) What's your sign? (CHUNK) Wanna ball? (CHUNK) This is my wee-wee. (CHUNK)

ANNOUNCER:	Aquario! The Earth Man. From Cartell Industries. Batteries not available.
ANNOUNCER:	This is KWKW-T-TV, Channel One, Cretin Oak, Vermont. At the tone — (TONE) — the tone will be 11 A.M.
SPORTS:	Tonight! Surprise international competition! The Pan Am Devil Dogs battle the Trans World Tigers over Milwaukee — come 11 on 7!
SOUND:	CLICK!
DANNY:	...issus Carolyn Presky, you've sold out! Now, let's see what you've bought on this — your third day on Hawaiian Sell-Out!
MUSIC:	HARP MELODY — GASPS AND APPLAUSE FROM CROWD
DANNY:	Oh, what a wise buy it was! 300 pounds of Chef Antoine's Southern Fried Glimps — toasted to frozen perfection, cubed, reheated and returned to water before you're ready. And the inside is just as lovely! Two shelves, where none are needed! Close the door and the light stays on!
CROWD:	APPLAUSE
DANNY:	How do you feel, Mrs. Presky?
MRS. P:	Ah — sick...
DANNY:	You can afford it — but like the Good Book says — "There's bigger deals to come." Bob, what's Mrs. Presky's heap so far?
BOB:	Right, Jack! So far, a complete broken set of color bars for the new home. Leveled mountain skis, and water rollers for that fun-filled open season. An unattached Grid-5 standup reheater, with a smoke window. And, of course, the refrigerated glimps!

CROWD:	APPLAUSE
DANNY:	Fair enough and fine enough for a queen. Over eight thousand World Bank Dummy Credits worth of hard-earned prizes. But — here we go! The pit is opening again...
MRS. P:	This is when I get the feeling...
DANNY:	Are you ready to trust your luck and sell it all out for this Mystery Deal?
CROWD:	YELLS ENCOURAGEMENT
MRS. P:	I'll keep what I've got.
CROWD:	NO! NO!
MRS. P:	All right, all right. I'll sell.
CROWD:	CHEERS
DANNY:	You've Sold Out, Mrs. Presky — for this unbelievable Mystery Deal. Here it is. Just open it up.
MRS. P:	But this — this is a bag of shit...
DANNY:	But it's very righteous shit! And according to New York prices, you've Made a Deal!!!
CROWD:	CHEERS
MUSIC:	KAZOO SIGNATURE OUT
WAYNE:	Hi! This is Wayne Boone, to ask you this important question. Who are you? Many people, believe it or not, don't. And, what's more, can't. Why?
ANNOUNCER:	That's easy, Wayne! They're suffering from Multiple Identity, Wayne. M.I. —
ECHOES:	THE WASTER!!

ANNOUNCER:	Yes, the ingestion of fatal toxins into the system has been shown to be directly responsible — indeed indirectly responsible — in more than 100 percent of all the cases on record. And their files are growing daily!
WAYNE:	So remember those pledges, and honor them, during this — Multiple Identity Year.
ANNOUNCER:	Thanks...
WAYNE:	Year.
ANNOUNCER:	Thanks, Wayne. Remember — M.I. —
ECHOES:	THE WASTER!!
ANNOUNCER:	Can strike anyone, anywhere, at any time. At home, in the office, or where you work!
SOUND:	CLICK!
BOB BASELINE:	...ends, this one won't go bad like the whole beef halves, or emit harmful radiation like the TVs. Trust Bob Baseline, friends! No weird noises like in those French tires I offed — I made available to you last February. No disease factor, like in the Atomic Grub Farms...
SOUND:	CLICK!
MUSIC:	XYLOPHONE THEME
TENOR:	End of Son...!
ANNOUNCER:	END OF SONG — the timeless story of the little people, striving to make a piepond of tranquility in a dirty, self-conscious hamlet that accepts neither, but rejects both! Brought to you every day by Bree!
SINGERS:	Bree! Bree! Bree! Clean! Clean! Clean!
VOICE:	Cleaner than anything!

ANNOUNCER:	And now the END OF SONG...
MUSIC:	HARP TRANSITION
PUBLIC ADDRESS:	(DING DING) Will the real Dr. Jergenson report to neurosurgery immediately! (DING)
INTERN:	Doctor? Doctor?
CARSTAIRS:	What is it?
INTERN:	Dr. Carstairs, I've got to talk to you.
CARSTAIRS:	I'm not Dr. Carstairs, my boy.
INTERN:	I've got to talk to *someone*, Dad.
CARSTAIRS:	Well, then, talk to me, Dr. ... Carstairs.
INTERN:	I'm having trouble identifying Mrs. Wilson's seminal vesicle and...
CARSTAIRS:	Perhaps if you spent less time in obstetrics with Nurse Warren and more time on the golf course with your probation officer... Well, do you remember what we talked about at the lake last summer?
INTERN:	Gee, Dad — I told you I was sorry then, and I'm sorry now.
CARSTAIRS:	(PAUSE) Does Peggy know that?
INTERN:	(TAKE) Who's Peggy?
BOTH:	(TAKE)
MUSIC:	HARP TRANSITION
ANNOUNCER:	We'll be back to END OF SONG after this timely message...
VOICE OVER:	Comedian Mrs. J.B. of Pine Barren, New Jersey,

	doesn't know our Napalm Olive camera is focused on HER...
MRS:	No. It's true. You see — my husband is a policeman, and you wouldn't believe how dirty he gets my clothes. I mean it. It's unbelievable.
VOICE OVER:	Oh, but we believed Mrs. P.Q. and listen to her reaction...
MRS:	I worry about it all night sometimes, you know? I hate to admit it — look at this horrible stain — sometimes I think my kids are doing it on purpose.
SOUND:	SIREN RING
SGT:	Nothin's on purpose, ma'am!
MRS:	Who are you?
SGT:	Sergeant Schvincter of the Dirt Patrol. Our mission — to keep America clean. And when the job gets this dirty, there's only one weapon! New Napalm Olive — with enzyme active BREE, from Germany!
MRS:	But, Sergeant! Look at my family — you'll never get them clean. They're colored!
SGT:	Negative, ma'am. With new Napalm Olive, even those sneaky little yellow stains just melt away. Stand back!
SOUND:	WHUMP AND FLAMES
MRS:	That's marvelous! All that dirt gone — and my family too! Wait 'til I tell my mother!
MUSIC:	HARP TRANSITION OUT
SOUND:	CLICK!
DANNY DOLLAR:	Hello? Mrs. Presky? This is Danny Dollar, and it's Lucky Dollar time for you.

MRS P:	What?
DANNY DOLLAR:	Are you watching me on TV?
MRS P:	No.
DANNY DOLLAR:	What are you doing?
MRS P:	Masturbating.
DANNY DOLLAR:	Oh. Go turn on your TV, darling.
MRS P:	Okay. (PUTS DOWN PHONE — WALKS OFF — WALKS BACK — PICKS UP PHONE)
DANNY DOLLAR:	You're watching Lucky Dollars now, Mrs. Presky?
MRS P:	Yes. You're the negro.
DANNY DOLLAR:	Don't I wish! No, you've got the wrong channel, Mrs. P.
MRS P:	Wait a minute. (PUTS DOWN PHONE — WALKS OFF — WALKS BACK — PICKS UP PHONE) Hello. Okay. You're the one holding the phone.
DANNY DOLLAR:	Right. Ready to win Lucky Dollars?
MRS P:	What?
DANNY DOLLAR:	Here we go. Here comes your Lucky Picture.
SOUND:	TIME BEATS AND BUZZER
DANNY DOLLAR:	Okay, Mrs. Caroline Presky of Palooka Lake, how many lucky baskets do you see?
MRS P:	I'm blind.
DANNY DOLLAR:	Then how did you know I was a negro? (PAUSE) Mrs. Presky? Mrs. Presky?...

MRS P:	Aw, fuck you! (HANGUP BUZZ)
ANNOUNCER:	This is KWKW-T-TV, Channel One, Gateway to the blue Pacific, Oceanside, Arizona. Get set for laughs on Corset Corners, when Mr. Whipple finds Dagwood lying down on top of Betty and Veronica — next on Nine!
SOUND:	CLICK!
SLOAT:	...Hey! I'm Ed Sloat, and you'll catch me on the ropes at 6 o'clock tonight on TAKE A DIVE — the all-family fight game. (SOCK!) Ahh! Oh! Don't miss me! (SOCK!)
MUSIC:	TAPED LOVE THEME
BOB:	Hello, friends, and welcome to the wonderful world of travel and adventure. Come with us as we visit strange places on THE GOLDEN HIND.
MUSIC:	QUICK OUT
BOB:	Hi, friends. I'm Bob Hind. Today, I'd like you to meet two of my dearest friends — George and Ida Matetsky...
GEORGE:	Good evening.
IDA:	Hello there.
BOB:	Well, George — you're just back from a really wonderful trip to...
THEY SPEAK TOGETHER:	
GEORGE:	To New Guinea, Bob.
IDA:	Peru, Bob.
BOB:	That's right. Honduras. And I understand that you and your lovely wife have brought back some beautiful color films for us to see here.

GEORGE:	No that's right, Bob.
BOB:	And we're gonna let you tell us all about it — right now.
MUSIC:	CUE IN
BOB:	What are those, Ida? Are those the natives?
IDA:	Yes, Bob — this is the Orinoco River — probably the largest river in the...
BOB:	Ah! And those are those towers you were telling me about, aren't they, George?
GEORGE:	Yes, they are. They're centuries old.
BOB:	That one looks a little different...
GEORGE:	Yes, Bob. That one doesn't have a bottom.
IDA:	Oh, George — will you ever forget those romantic clam fishermen?
GEORGE:	What romantic clam fishermen, Ida?
BOB:	Uh — we'll be back to part two of THE GOLDEN HIND.
MUSIC:	CUTS OUT
NICK:	Hi, everybody. I'm Nick Gunderson, out at Gunderson's Famous Furniture — 14019 McKissick, three blocks west of the airport at Old Oildale Highway. We're announcing the greatest bargain bonanza in our 17-year history. Our giant Rodeo Days sale is now going on.
MUSIC:	TAPED THEME IN AND UNDER
NICK:	Just look at this! 15 rooms of factory-fresh Greek Provincial furniture — 14 pieces in all — only 89.99. And remember, with every Futura Dinette

	Ensemble you buy this weekend, Uncle Tom Gunderson would like you to have either this nationally advertised all-Formica bacon baster, or this completely-framed, oil on velvet pitcher, called The Crying Clowns, by Bernard of Holly...
SOUND:	CLICK!
SECRETARY:	Do you mean to tell us, Admiral Groat, that when your men aren't firing at something, they can go down below decks and learn to play the blues?
MURMUR — GAVEL	
ADMIRAL:	These men are being fired UPON, too, Mr. Secretary. These are brave men. Don't forget that.
SECRETARY:	But Admiral — you can't count the times our own men fire on our own men as real action. They don't get paid for it.
ADMIRAL:	Mr. Secretary, I killed three men yesterday. My own. Now don't you think I have a right to sing the blues?
SECRETARY:	That's not the —
SOUND:	CLICK!
OZZIE:	But Uncle Henry'll be here any minute, and I just can't let him see me like this!
SOUND:	LAUGHTER
NEAL THE HORSE:	Ozzie! That's my hat!
SOUND:	LAUGHTER AND APPLAUSE
ANNOUNCER:	Tune in again tomorrow at 5:30 for another hilarious adventure of OZZIE KNOWS FATHER. This is Channel 9 — KWKW-T-TV in No Heart, Colorado — the Town Without a Heart.

SOUND:	MARCHING FEET — MECHANICAL SOUNDS
VOICE:	Shoes for Industry!
VOICE 2:	Shoes for the dead!
VOICE:	Shoes for Industry!
JOE:	Hi, I'm Joe Beets. Hey, what chance does a returning deceased war veteran have for that good-paying job, more sugar and the free mule you've been dreaming of? Think it over. Then, take off your shoes. Now, you can see how increased spending opportunities means harder work for everyone. And more of it, too! So do your part today — join with millions of your neighbors and turn in your shoes —
VOICE:	For industry!
ANNOUNCER:	Passengers on board a wooden ship begin to suspect each other is crazy until a strangeness covers them like a shrouded forehock on EARTHLIGHT MOVIE tonight at 11:30.
PRENSKY:	Howdy, folks — this is Carl Prensky, with a word from the Xerox corporation. With a word from the Xerox corporation. Just because your old friends at the Flying Roman Oil Company have changed their name to FROMCO — the petroleum products division of ACNE-CIVILUX — doesn't mean that we're not givin' you the same old gas — and games too. This month, collect the heads of the Presidents...
SOUND:	CLICK!
MUSIC:	XYLOPHONE THEME
ANNOUNCER:	The ABC D Goldfish Television Network presents the following program in colors.

VOICE OVER:	Erect from our newsroom in the Moon, the ABC D Goldfish Evening News. With Walter Klondike — and Bill Ding in New New Ork — Flash Gordon at the White House — and George Matetsky, on Earth. And now — the nudes.
WALTER:	Good evening. The most remarkable medical achievement of modern times has entered its fourth successful day. Here, with a report from Whittier Crater, is ABC D Goldfish correspondent, Felix Paparazzi. Felix?

INTERMITTENT DROPOUTS THROUGHOUT THE INTERVIEW

FELIX:	Here at General Hershey General Hospital, America's first man-made baby, Adam 13, is developing far beyond the expectations of Surrogate General Klein and his medical staff. Dr. General, sir — how is Adam 13 progressing?
GENERAL:	We are quite frankly astonished at the rate of cellular progression.
FELIX:	I realize that antiseptic security precautions must be maintained, but when will we be able to actually see him?
GENERAL:	Surely not before his growth rate stabilizes.
FELIX:	How many inches is he now?
GENERAL:	As of an hour ago — 148. That's lunar feet. He has a full head of hair, his features are normal in every respect — and pleasing too, I might add. Our only concern now is with a certain pigmentation imbalance which has manifested in the last day.
FELIX:	Is that serious, Dr. General?
GENERAL:	No, not serious. It's a matter of personal taste.
WALTER:	Adam 13's incipient negritude will come as a pleasant surprise to his Honorary Aquarian parents — Ralph

	Bunche and Ida Lupino. In other news, final steps were taken in or near Washington to secure the merger of the U.S. Government with TMZ General Corp. This former zinc bushing agency thus will become the wealthiest industry listed on the heavy metal board. Over 100 billion world bank dummy credit write-offs.
SOUND:	PLATES & CUTLERY
JOYCE:	Bye now!... Whew! They're all gone. Madge, will you help me put what's left of the Chicken à la King back into the fridge?
MADGE:	Honestly, Joyce — I don't know where you get the energy. 14 children, President of the World Bank — and you still find time to make the best buffet in Fresno. I can remember when the least little problem put you right to sleep.
JOYCE:	Not anymore, Madge — not since I discovered a simple little pill called METHEDRINE!
ANNOUNCER:	METHEDRINE — available without a prescription at drug centers everywhere. Remember — METHEDRINE carries the Seal of Approval of the Armenian Medical Association.
ANOTHER ANNOUNCER:	This is KWKW-T-TV in Gourd of Ashes, Wyoming. Poopie Whipple joins Happy tonight on The Happy Hamburger Show at 11:15...
SINGERS:	(TO "BONANZA" THEME — WITH KAZOO) BUMPITY, BUMPITY, BUMPITY, BUMP, BANANA! BUMPITY, BUMPITY, BUMPITY, BUMPITY, BUMPITY BUMP BUMP BUMP! HEY! (REPEAT)
SOUND:	BIRDS
L'IL SLOP:	Hey, thar, Hoss! You pick up them duck hats and

meet Pappy and Jeeter down by the poultry punch!...

(THE SOUND IS TURNED DOWN)

AD LIB BREAK — TV GLIDE LISTINGS — THEN SEGUE TO:

DAVID:	Look! The movies are on! (HE TURNS UP THE SOUND)
ANNOUNCER:	...ollowing program is brought to you in colors.
MUSIC:	HARP THEME
ANNOUNCER 2:	EVERYNIGHT AT THE MOVIES — 52 fabulous features every day, all day, eight days a week. Tonight? A tender story of love defiled — Lily Lamont and Eerpo Sweeny star as MOTHER AND CHILD.
VOICE:	They weren't the same size! They weren't even the same sex! Could they make it together? MOTHER AND CHILD. F. Scott Firesign's daring indictment of reality blazes to the screen in a flush of cleanliness.
ANNOUNCER 2:	Brought to you tonight by...
SOUND:	FOOTBALL — CROWD
MUSIC:	XYLOPHONE
ED:	Hi, I'm Ed White of the Chicago Beasts. You know, smashin' skulls on the gridiron is nothin' compared to drinkin' three of these little mothers. They gonna twist yo' head up so tight! Take it from me, Jim —
JIM:	Thanks!
ED:	— nothin' beats getting' stoned on Golden Spook Wipe-Out Malt Liquor!
SOUND:	CLICK!

ANNOUNCER:	A man goes looking for a memory — and can't remember where he left it. See the ROUND WORLD OF SQUEEKY WHITTAKER tonight at ten...
SOUND:	CLICK!
ANNOUNCER:	Sgt. Bradshaw takes his wife with an electric knife at 10:30 tonight on CARHOOK!...
SOUND:	CLICK!
TINGLING:	But darn it, Dean Torture! They can't get away with this! You come over to this window right now!
DEAN:	Yes, President Tingling.
TINGLING:	What are all those crazy students doing in the Groat Memorial Swimming Pool?
DEAN:	Swimming, sir.
TINGLING:	Well, they're doing it in a crazy manner and I'm calling the police!
SOUND:	CLICK!
ROCKY:	You fuels! Haven't you found the contract yet? Your time is almost up!
CATHERWOOD:	Rococo! You slimy blackmailer! How did you get in here? You don't have a key.
ROCKY:	No, only half a key...
SOUND:	CLICK!
GENERALISSIMO:	Relax, Sr. "Smeeth" — we are both civilized men.
SMITH:	Can I have my hat back then?
GENERALISSIMO:	Sure.

PREZ:	Lemme kill him, boss!
GENERALISSIMO:	Take it easy, President Nixon. Now — why does a not-bad lookin' young Jankee like jorself risk his kneck for a silly democratic principle like money?
SMITH:	I'm not working for money, Generalissimo. I'm working for a comp...
SOUND:	CLICK!
PATRICK:	I am not a number — I am a free...
SOUND:	CLICK!
MUSIC:	HARP BEEPS
ANNOUNCER:	The Bigtown News gets it together tonight at 11 P.M. Professor Andy Gerkin rips the burg apart to bring you the freshest national news on the market!
ANDY:	Jap discovers planet, thousands muse! Tonight with Bernice Yakamoto...
ANNOUNCER:	Barbara Bobo eats up Hollywood and spits it right back out!
BARBARA:	What nameless baby was seen in high boots and no pants in bed last night at a famous night club... (FADES OUT)
ANNOUNCER:	Tom Redman — a tough guy with a tougher message!
TOM:	So let's all remember that we mustn't run in the house, and tomorrow morning the North Sector of the city will have a full-dress white-glove inspection. That'll be a lot of fun!
ANNOUNCER:	Tonight! Eleven! The Tom Redman Mailpouch News. It can't happen here!
SOUND:	CLICK!

SINGER.	Cyclamate Scoreboard! Cyclamate Scoreboard! Let's see how our team did today...
ANNOUNCER:	Awww! The Angels lose tonight — 5 to 3 in a twi-double-header-nite to the Devils at Rogers Field in Hell.
SINGER:	You never lose with Cyclamate It really rings the bell!
SOUND:	DING
SOUND:	CLICK!
LOUISE:	Assassination is funny Plain folks'll do it for money You may think I'm being funny But watch out — (BANG) — they'll get you!

APPLAUSE

HAPPY HAMBURGER:	Thanks Louise. You'll be taking off your clothes in San Diego — is that right?

ETC. — OPEN IMPROV — HUCKSTER CUES HAPPY FOR COMMERCIAL

HAPPY HAMBURGER:	Do I have to do this now?
HUCKSTER:	Las Vegas! Now! Eat! Drink! Fight! Three days! Four nights! At Archie Pelago's EL PLASTICO! Now appearing nightly at the Lizard Lounge — the Finger Sisters! And our giant splash-tacular on the Roman Revolving Stage — Neil Armstrong and Madam Nu's Big Tet Holiday Review! Las Vegas! Glamour Weekend. Twenty-seven-fifty! (SOTTO) Friday and Saturday not included. Sundays extra.
HAPPY HAMBURGER:	...back. Jackie, you were in your wife lately, weren't you?

ETC. — OPEN IMPROV

LOUISE:	I'd just like to say hello to my mother! (GIVES HER THE FINGER)
HAPPY HAMBURGER (ON CUE):	Do I have to do that? We'll be back in just a minute, but first, here's a word from AIRBEER.
ANNOUNCER:	No, Earth is no place to live — but it sure is a swell spot to brew beer. It's that old-fashioned air down there that makes the difference. So...
SOUND:	CLICK!
ANNOUNCER:	...ext, a stutterer wins the Medal of Honor in a thrilling wartime saga — B-B-B-BEYOND HELP! On Super Cha...
SOUND:	CLICK!
REVEREND F:	...you know, freedom's a wonderful, but dangerous thing? You know, dear friends, when Mrs. Ferberger and I were down Earthside last spring on a free-world-wide mission for God, we saw this so-called hippie "freedom". Yes, Mrs. Ferberger actually threw up on my coat...
SOUND:	CLICK!
VERONICA:	Darn! If we'd only evacuated along with the others, Orgie, none a this woulda happened!
BETTY:	Orgie, we'll be waiting for you at the high school. Promise you'll come back in one piece!
ORGIE:	I promise!
SOUND:	BOOM
ANNOUNCER:	ECHO) Aames Guns! (ECHO OFF) Arms? Firearms? Bang-bangs? Go to Aames Guns at 2234117 E. Military Highway in Palooka! Ed aims to please and so does Louise. Don't hide arms — get sidearms at AAMES GUNS!!!!!

GIRL:	Daddy? Where can I get a good deal in a Christian Atmosphere?
ANNOUNCER:	Joe Beets Realty in Yucaipa! That's where! Big acreage? Bigger savings. Deals for you! Yes, Joe Beets fought in the Big One and wants you to get in on the action. Indian land a go-go! At JOE BEETS REALITY, 227 E. Rhode Island School of Design Terrace in Yucaipa!
GIRL:	(ECHO) Real negro hair!!!!
ANNOUNCER:	Rastus Afro Hair Dealers — Uptown! You're uptight in your Rastus au natural soul wig from MISTAH BEE OF HARLEM.
YUKAMOTO:	Hi. I'm Henry Yukamoto, owner of Yukamoto School of Music. What's life without music? A drag, man.
GIRL (SINGS):	It's Yuka-moto!
ANNOUNCER:	Right, Henry! Yukamoto Schools of Music doesn't force music into children.
YUKAMOTO:	Yes. It forces it out of them.
ANNOUNCER:	Yuk — Yuk — Yukamoto Schools of Music! Good deals in a Christian atmosphere!
SOUND:	CLICK!
ED:	Hello. This is Ed White of the Central Division of the United Government. With the enemy everywhere, we've had to do some hard thinking about zinc. Zinc about it. That's not very funny if you know there's enough zinc in your system to kill a man. For what? Release it. And if there's a Government around, we'll all be the richer.
ANNOUNCER:	This has been a public cervix message from HELP — the Heavy Metal Environmental Leg Police, New New York, Topside.

ANNOUNCER 2:	Stay tuned for the Boiled Owl Movie as a young couple finds out that getting a baby means some changes in their sleeping arrangements on GET YOUR HANDS OFF ME!...
SOUND:	CLICK!
FATHER O'LONG:	Like soft rounded dark furry things humping together in the night. Oh, heavenly grid — guide us under dark and troubled waters, and help us to comprehend the incomprehensible, even though we can never understand it...
SOUND:	CLICK!
ANKERMAN:	...discussion of educational opportunities in the negro industry is the Very Reverend Deacon...
SOUND:	CLICK!
FATHER GROAT:	...his mouth has been twisted to one side, but now is back in place. Oh, heavenly Grid — it's getting so you can't tell the ACs from the DCs — as it says in Timothy 2, Chapter 7 — "And they came down from the heights, yet where were they to plug it in?" We all get exhausted with a manifold of worries. I think we all long for a master cylinder, who can turn on some stopping power! Yes, a humbler...
SOUND:	CLICK!
BOB BASELINE:	...or spurt fire like the hoses. No, friends, no overheating like the tropical fishes. This one won't take over the house like the high-speed vibrator clocks. No, fr...
SOUND:	CLICK!
FATHER O'LONG:	...pour oil on troubled waters. No! Rather let us stand Humble, seeking, through the Rich Field of Mobil American thinking, a new and better Standard — our Chevron flashing bright — we'll

bridge the Gulf and communicate at last with this Shell we call life...

SOUND: CLICK!

WAR BACKGROUND

DRUGHEAD: ...en why do they want to kill all us kids, Betty?

BETTY: Oh, they're just jealous because they think they're gonna die, Drughead!

DRUGHEAD: Gee, whiz, Betty! Don't adults remember about having a lot of fun and living forever?

SOUND: CLICK!

ANNOUNCER: ...olden Spook Wipeout Malt Liq...

SOUND: CLICK!

REVEREND F: ...anks to Brother Wayne Johnson out at Eisenhower Crater for his good wishes for Mrs. Ferberger's continued trouble with the batteries for her heart and many other...

SOUND: CLICK!

ANNOUNCER: All right Mrs. Presky — would you rather hit this Jew over the head with a bag of sugar, or beat out that rhythm on a drum?

SOUND: CLICK!

HAPPY: ...o I have to do this now? All right. New Napal...

SOUND: CLICK!

JOEY: ...ave to do this now? All right. New Napal...

SOUND: CLICK!

HUCKSTER: ...as Vegas! Eat! Drink! Fight! Six excitin...

SOUND:	CLICK!
MERV:	...uess I have to do this now, right?...
SOUND:	CLICK!
SINGER:	(STAR-SPANGLED BANNER)
SOUND:	CLICK!
WAR NOISES	
BETTY:	...ou all right, Orgie? You aren't hurt are you?
DRUGHEAD:	Orgie, ol' pal! Say you're okay like you promised!
VERONICA:	Look out kids! Here comes another wave...
SOUND:	CLICK!
SINGER:	(STAR-SPANGLED BANNER)
SOUND:	CLICK!
SOUND:	WHITE NOISE
SOUND:	CLICK
HAROLD:	It's a Ferberger! I'm not kidding, Manny. It's a Ferberger! They're worth fortunes!
MANNY:	What is?
HAROLD:	Ferbergers.
MANNY:	(PAUSE) No shit! Let's go!
SOUND:	CLICK!
VERONICA:	...e thought you were dead, Orgie.
ORGIE:	Heck no, Veronica! Reggie slipped some STP in my malt!

DRUGHEAD:	Gee, that's a bummer.
ORGIE:	It sure was — for the first three days. But it gave me one heck of an idea!
BETTY:	What is it, Orgie? There isn't much time like this left!
ORGIE:	Here's my plan, kids. We'll make Mrs. Grundy the Corn Maiden. Then Drughead, disguised as Mescalito, will go tell Mr. Witherspoon his real name, while Betty and Veronica...
SOUND:	CLICK!
RALPH ONE:	Hiya, friends, Ralph...
SOUND:	CLICK!
RALPH TWO:	Hiya, friends, Ralph...
SOUND:	CLICK!
RALPH THREE:	Hiya, friends, Ralph...
SOUND:	CLICK!
RALPH SPOILSPORT:	Hiya, friends, Ralph Spoilsport, owner and operator of the world's biggest dealership, west of Baalbek. As you know, we're overdosed again with all tastes and kilos. Let's just take a look at some of these fabulous lids... The LaGuardia Report says this pound should be copped for 10 thousand five hundred dollars, in easy monthly sentences of a year to life and nobody down. Our complete price to you, including sticks and stems and seeds, wine-soaked and sugar-cured, completely clean for your smoking pleasure, the complete price, only what the traffic will allow in unmarked bills, delivered to me, Ralph Icebag, in a plain brown wrapper, by a brown-shoed square in the dead of night. Let's take a taste of this fabulous Yucatan Blue, scored to you from the sky-blue waters of

that beautiful Mexican bay — hand-picked by naked little brown native boys, in their tight leather aprons, running through the fields by the sea o and the sea crimson sometimes like fire and the glorious sunsets and the fig trees in the Alameda gardens yes yes and all the queer little streets and pink and blue and yellow houses and the rose gardens and the jessamine and geraniums and cactuses and Gibraltar as a girl (boy) where I was a flower of the mountains yes where I put the rose in my (her) hair like the Andalusian girls used yes and how he (she) kissed me under the Moorish wall and I thought well as well him (her) as another and he (she) asked me would I yes to say yes my mountain flower and first I put my arms around him (her) yes and drew him (her) down to me so he (I) could feel my (her) breasts all perfumed yes and his (her) heart was going like mad and yes I said yes I will yes...yes...yes.

SOUND: CLICK!

MUTT 'N' SMUTT

This is the first episode of a long-lived series inspired by Phil Proctor's love of crazy catalogs, from which a list of bizarre products would be ordered and shipped by two squabbling storekeepers. Introduced at the Ash Grove in November 1970, the characters have appeared many times since on stage, XM Satellite Radio and NPR. It's essentially a Vaudeville sketch from the age of blackface and "rube" comics with a nod to Forties radio's "Lum and Abner" and "Amos 'n' Andy."

ORIGINAL CAST
Phil Austin as Tarface Pork

Peter Bergman as Doodie Fenster

David Ossman as Smutt

Phil Proctor as Mutt

MUTT 'N' SMUTT

RADIO VOICE: This is KOKE, San Francisco — the Blue Network Station for the Northern and Central Valleys. The time is 9:01.

RADIO VOICE 2: Coast to coast, from New York . . .

RADIO VOICE 3: Chicago . . .

RADIO VOICE 4: Detroit . . .

VOICE 3: Moscow . . .

VOICE 2: Palo Alto . . .

VOICE 1: The Blue Network of affiliated stations all over America present the following program direct from WLSM and WFST, Cincinatti, Ohio — Here's Mutt 'n' Smutt!

MUSIC AND APPLAUSE SIGN

ANNOUNCER: It's time again for those nice Driml People to bring you the Mutt 'n' Smutt Show! Yes, folks, Mutt 'n' Smutt, those gamey old pros of the con game, cornholed — er, holed up in their corner store, just a stone's throw from City Hall, on the shady side of the street in Mixville, USSA . . .

SMUTT: (MUMBLING) . . . 200 gross glow-in-the-dark duck hats, two crates biodegradable stoat-humpers . . .

MUTT: (OFF) Smutt!

SMUTT:	What, Mutt?
MUTT:	(OFF) Did we get that order of wolf stools in from the Chinese trader on Cock Bridge?
SMUTT:	Did ya look under the Tyrolean Shoe Stretchers from Guam?
MUTT:	(OFF) Yep. No wolf stools.
SMUTT:	Did ya look back there by the nails?
MUTT:	(OFF) Toe nails or finger nails?
SMUTT:	You know the back room as well as I do, Mutt.
MUTT:	(OFF) I used to, but some jackass put the shipment of pepperoni and mushroom ice-cream next to the irradiated fish. There's an ice-cream lagoon back there.
SMUTT:	Thank goodness the mercury don't change the color of the ice-cream.
MUTT:	That don't matter . . . just get them papers ready to send back those wolf stools. Gov'ment says they're faulty.
SMUTT:	Faulty?! That's crazy, Mutt. Gov'ment don't never say nothin's ever faulty — they're subversive!
MUTT:	Same thing, Smutt, same thing. We cain't sell 'em or you know what'll happen.
SMUTT:	Well, that's no problem! I'll just change the name on the crate to Fenster Indian School and send 'em along with the irradiated ice-cream.
MUTT:	I thought we was gonna send 'em the melted crayons.
SMUTT:	Them little Injun kids'll never know the difference.

THE TELEPHONE RINGS. SMUTT PICKS IT UP.

SMUTT:	Oh, diddle! Hello? Mutt 'n' Smutt. Smutt speakin', Mutt's in the back.
DOODIE (ON PHONE):	Hello, Mutt?
SMUTT:	Oh, howdy, Doodie. It's Doody Fenster, Mutt.
MUTT:	Good luck.
SMUTT:	What is it, Miz Fenster? I got a whole shitload of work piled up here and I . . .
DOODIE (PHONE):	Please, Mutt! I don't know where to turn! I'm so upset about my daughter, little Judy!
SMUTT:	That purty little thing?
DOODY (PHONE):	Won't do her hygiene homework, won't wear a diaphragm, won't drive on the freeway, won't argue with Daddy Fenster about the War! I'm tellin' you, Mutt, Daddy and I have ev'ry reason to believe that that purty young piece of ours is mentally demanged . . .
SMUTT:	De-manged?
MUTT:	What did you say, Smutt?
SMUTT:	I said, she said "demanged."
DOODIE (PHONE):	Did I? I meant to say de-ranged!
SMUTT:	You really need help, Miz Fenster. Have you seen the Doc?
DOODIE (PHONE):	See the duck? That quack?
SMUTT:	Yeah, the duck, Miz Fenster. Goodbye.

HE HANGS UP THE PHONE.

MUTT:	The duck?
SMUTT:	Mutt?

MUTT:	What?
SMUTT:	I think you oughtter stop dating Judy. Her mother's catchin' on . . .
MUTT:	I wonder who she caught it from?

THE DOORBELL RINGS, DOOR OPENS AND TARFACE ENTERS.

TARFACE:	Hello, dare, MuttsnSmutts, yuk yuk yuk . . .
SMUTT:	Well, if it ain't Tarface Pork.

APPLAUSE CUE.

MUTT:	Hi, Tarface. Your Mistress send you?
TARFACE:	Oh, yeah! I'se crazy 'bout her! But I ain't got no time fo' cheese-loggin' now — I'se woikin' fo' Miz Fenster.
SMUTT:	She needs all the help she can get . . .
TARFACE:	Yeah, 'specially now, she so prostate wif grease 'bout her daughter, slippery Judy. She all bent over 'bout it. She give me this list of things to pick up for the slaves' picnic an' lynchin' tomorrow.
MUTT:	That's "luncheon."
TARFACE:	Yeah, dat's right. I'se the ghost of honor!
SMUTT:	Is this on account?
TARFACE:	Yeah — on accounta Miz Doodie don't trust me wif cash! She 'fraid I'll spend it on yellow shoes and co-caine!
MUTT:	Don't matter what you spend it on, just spend it here.
TARFACE:	Yuk yuk yuk . . . Here de list — she want four minority frightening sticks, an artificial boiled owl, a six-pack of hooded velvet angels, some Danish flash cards, a litter of roll-over musical kittens, a chrome-style fish mask, and a genuine moleskin Tom Mix cowboy outfit.

SMUTT:	We're all outta them. Sent 'em to the Secret Service.
MUTT:	Shaddup! That's a secret!
TARFACE:	Oh, an' I been havin' a heap o' trouble wit' my ol' lady lately. Throw in a bottle of Dr. Bad's Witch Spray and put it on de MassaCharge! Yuk yuk yuk!

THE TELEPHONE RINGS. MUTT PICKS IT UP.

MUTT:	Mutt 'n' Smutt's. Mutt speakin' — Smutt's in the cryin' room.
DOODIE (PHONE):	Mutt, it's finally happened. Judy's in trouble and I don't know who else to turn on.
MUTT:	She's sex-crazed, Miz Fenster.
DOODIE (PHONE):	Don't play mind-games with me now, Mutt! Remember what you promised me that night, under the waterbed?
MUTT:	Oh, fer Cop's sake! Listen, Tarface — she wants to talk to you.
TARFACE:	That woman cain't resist me! Yuk yuk yuk.
DOODIE (PHONE):	Oh, Mutt! Judy's run away from home!
TARFACE:	Oh, yeah? Whatfo' she gone and done a dumb thing like dat fo'?
DOODIE (PHONE):	Well, she's been acting real upset-like ever since we put her pet hamsters to sleep.
TARFACE:	What? Wha'd you do that fo'?
DOODIE (PHONE):	You see, Daddy Fenster got her a walkin' catfish as a surprise for Easter, and he was afeared there wouldn't be near enough room in the garage for both of 'em, what with the hamsters multiplying like cheese . . .
TARFACE:	What did you say?

DOODIE (PHONE):	Like Chinese. And they're voracious eaters. So Daddy Fenster thought it would be best all around if we just put those dear little hamsters to sleep.
TARFACE:	Dat's weird!
DOODIE (PHONE):	So, t'other night he sung lullabies to them 'till they was fast aslumberin', then he scooped 'em up and packed 'em in the new Garbage Stomper . . .
TARFACE:	Great gracious me! You people certainly do keep up wif de now ecological times!
DOODIE (PHONE):	But Judy found out when she threw out the white trash this morning — and she upped and then she cleaned it up, and then she upped and ran away with the catfish.
TARFACE:	Oh, my Boint Cork!
DOODIE (PHONE):	And that catfish is dangerous! He eats electricity!
TARFACE:	Oh, my gracious! I'll sure tell Massas MuttsnSmutts to keep their eyes out for that fine fine superfine daughter of yours.
DOODIE (PHONE):	Well, who is this?
TARFACE:	Dis am de catfish! So long, white-fish.
MUTT:	Wha'd she want, Tarface?
TARFACE:	Oh, she jes' called up an' reminded me ta pick up another pair of yellow shoes, an' a Mr. Jim of West Hollywood lizard-skin loungin' jacket, an' a lady-size quarter-pound tube of Dr. Peeru's organic sniffin' powder.
SMUTT:	Yuk yuk yuk.

A MUSICAL TRANSITION.

DWIGHT YEAST:	We'll be back to the terrifying world of Mutt 'n' Smutt in just a moment, but first let's take a time out for . .

16 MEN:	Hello, Mr. Announcer . . .
YEAST:	Well, cut me up and fry me in lard! It's the 16 Talking Men!
16 MEN:	I'm hungry! What's for dinner?
YEAST:	The Majority's favorite! White bread, ground meat and sugar.
16 MEN:	What's for dessert?
YEAST:	Driml, naturally!
16 MEN:	Un-naturally good!
YEAST:	And unnaturally good for you, like all the fine pressed-wax and coal-tar desserts from those fine folks at Driml Foods.
16 MEN:	What about the Giant Cheese Log Giveaway?
YEAST:	Glad you reminded me! Yuk yuk yuk! With every little box of Driml's brand new flavors, you get a giant, Early–American cheese log, suitable for framing.
16 MEN:	What a wonderful gift, Dwight!
YEAST:	That's right. Why don't you tell our listeners about Driml's bland new Flavor Wheel?
16 MEN:	Okay! Strawberry — Cherry — Hairy — Road Apple — and Lime! And now — brbrbrbrbrbrbbrrrrr! Wool!
YEAST:	Thanks, boys!
16 MEN:	You're welcome, Dwight!
YEAST:	And this week, millions of cartons of Driml Desserts are being balloon-lifted into the Tennessee Valley. Yes, after the traditional Yule-tide floods, they'll be scooped up and pushed together by the Army Corps of

	Engineers to make mammoth electrical dams. Once again, Driml does its part to bring . . .
16 MEN:	More power to the people!
YEAST:	Right on, boys. And now, back to Mutt 'n' Smutt!

MUSICAL TRANSITION.

SMUTT:	Whew! That was the dang-blangest biggest order I ever did deliver!
MUTT:	Sure glad Doody took all of them Subversive Wolf Stools.
SMUTT:	What a nice lady. Now her wolves'll have something to sit down on!
MUTT:	Too bad about Daddy Fenster, tho'.
SMUTT:	Yep. That pack of mutant hamsters is worrying him to death.
MUTT:	Yeah. They come outta that Garbage Stomper more organized than ever . . .
SMUTT:	When aroused, those hamsters can swarm up over the hill like a cheese hoard . . .
MUTT:	A what?
SMUTT:	A Chinese whore!
MUTT:	Speakin' of Chinese — I think I know what happened to Judy.
SMUTT:	What?
MUTT:	Well, I figure she been havin' so many double-dates she come down with a case of the Schitzofreens! She didn't run away — she split!
SMUTT:	I hope it ain't catchin'.

MUTT:	Naw. It ain't a promiscuous disease.

MUTT 'N' SMUTT (TOGETHER): But one of us is gonna hafta stop seein' Judy!

MUTT:	Smutt?
SMUTT:	What?

THEME MUSIC COMES IN AND PLAYS UNDER.

MUTT:	I just had two terrible thoughts.
SMUTT:	'Bout what?
MUTT:	'Bout Judy. She's gonna make some man a fine couple someday.
SMUTT:	Yep.
MUTT:	Sun never sets on a steel hat.
SMUTT:	Yep. Sun never sets on a steel hat.

MUSIC UP AND UNDER.

YEAST:	You've been listening to the Mutt 'n' Smutt Show with Harry Truman as Mutt, Albin Barkeley as Smutt and J. Hoobert Heever as Tarface Pork. Tonight's special star, Eleanor Roosevelt as Doody Fenster. Be with us next week, same fire-time, same fire-station for the Mutt 'n' Smutt show.
MUTT:	Good night, Smutt.
SMUTT:	Good night, Mutt! Good night, everybody!

MUSIC UP. APPLAUSE CUE. MUSIC FADES OUT.

THE DR. BLOJOB SHOW

This script played briefly at the Ash Grove in November of the Depression year, 1970.

ORIGINAL CAST
Phil Austin as Marlo Hortebagy

Peter Bergman as Dr. Blojob

David Ossman as The Manager

Phil Proctor as the Hon. Bill Ding

THE DR. BLOJOB SHOW

THE THEATRE MANAGER COMES ON STAGE, BRINGING A MICROPHONE OUT WITH HIM FROM THE WINGS.

MANAGER: Hello? Hello? Is this working? Hello! Well, I guess to most of you I don't need any introduction. Gee, wasn't that a wonderful comedy co-feature? The ever-wonderful Harold Arlen and Fay Bainter as Mutt 'n' Smutt in "Mutt 'n' Smutt Burn Down The Farm!" You know, standing where I do, in the wings, I get a much different perspective on the movies. You know, from there Fay Bainter's nose looks a big as a truck . . . Yes, sir . . .

Tonight's big Feature, Porgie & Mudhead's latest laff-riot "High School Madness" will go on at 9:30, right on schedule . . .

Well, it's Wednesday night — Bingo Cash Night here at the Rialto and I'd like to congratulate last week's winner, Miss Virginia Creeper of Dutch Elm Street, who won last week, the 75-piece set of stainless steel dental equipment! That's enough for the whole family, isn't it, Miz Creeper? But — no Bingo tonight — but it's going to be all right! You read about it in the Rocket — tonight Mixville is proud to host the Regional Finals in the Bureau of Human Reclamation's most successful project on the Public Welfare.

Yes, friends, the Cross-Country Caravan stops in our town tonight. Yes, you're the Judge and you're the Jury as we welcome to our home stage — Dr. Manual Blojob!

DR. BLOJOB AND THE TWO CONTESTANTS ARE REVEALED CENTER STAGE.

DR. B: Yes, yes, yes, hello everybody!! You know who I am! Dr. Blojob . . .

THE TWO CONTESTANTS JOIN IN SINGING THE DOCTOR'S THEME SONG TO THE TUNE OF "MR. SANDMAN":

CONTESTANTS: Dr. Blojob,
Send me a job!
I'm out of work and
I feel like a slob! . . .

DR. B: Yes, that's our theme tonight and every night, and heck, let's admit it, that's why you're here tonight. You wouldn't be watching this harmless entertainment if you had a job. Everybody's out of it nowadays — 'cept me — and that's my job — getting you back to work! And I think we've done a pretty good job so far.

APPLAUSE CUE

Yes, your applause is going to make it or break it tonight for these semi-finalists in the Southern Ohio Valley Regional Human Reclamation Run-Offs. The winner of tonight's Sudden Death Talent Exposition will go to work instantly, as a Garbage Dispenser at the Steubenville Mole-Preening Works at a dollar-three an hour!

APPLAUSE CUE

MANAGER: Dr. Blojob — here's your first contestant and finalist. He's our local defending Champion and our good friend, Marlo Hortebagy!

APPLAUSE CUE — MARLO ENTERS, WEARING A DUCK MASK

DR. B: By the look of that shabby suit, Marlo, you evidently held a position of some importance . . .

MARLO: Yes, Doc. But it slipped through my fingers like everything else in those dark days.

DR. B: What did you do then? It looks to me like you spent a lot of time on your hands and knees . . .

MARLO: Close, Doc — but nothing that big. I was only the President of Southern Ohio's largest regional bank — The Tri-City Chemical Groat and Pig Exchange Bank in Cincinatti.

APPLAUSE CUE

DR. B: Well, I guess after the deflation, your life must have passed you right by!

MARLO: Yes, indeed. That's beautiful, Doc. But it didn't make such a pretty picture from where I sat. Yes, right after my wife Daisy left me, they turned my Bank into a discotheque.

DR. B: Well, this is it, Marlo. You know you're up against a pretty strong opponent. This is the Finals, so either you win or you go on Relief! What are you going to do for us tonight?"

MARLO: "Way down upon the Swanee River," Doc.

DR. B: Well, with a magnetic personality like that, Marlin, I could leave you here all night to charm the folks.

MARLO: Don't leave me out here all alone, Dr. Blojob! Not in the Duck Mask!

MANAGER: They're all your friends out there, Marlo.

MARLO: No, they aren't! They stole my Bank!

MARLO, ABANDONED ON STAGE, GETS IT TOGETHER AND PERFORMS HIS SONG AND DANCE. IT'S WHAT YOU'D EXPECT FROM A BANK PRESIDENT.

APPLAUSE CUE

DR. B: Well, Norman, what did that performance register on the Laff-o-Graff?

MANAGER:	A big 137, Dr. Blojob!
DR. B:	Well, that's only three points away from last year's championship drill team, The Aristocrats. But there's some stiff competition coming up.
MANAGER:	That's right, Dr. B. And here he is — the District of Columbia Regional Champ — an odds-on sentimental favorite! He's been here once before — and how can we forget that! — so come on out — the Honorable William Ding, former President of the United Snakes!

APPLAUSE CUE — BILL DING ENTERS, WEARING A MASK

DR. B:	(EMBRACING DING) Bill, I don't suppose anybody but the very young out there could forget you!
DING:	Yes, I'll never live it down.
DR. B:	Is that why you wear that mask, Bill?
DING:	He he he! No, I only wear this mask for theatrical effect — as a gag — and when I rob discotheques.
DR. B:	How we remember that Presidential wit! What a great distance you've come! Where else could so many people from so many different social background, ways of life, and postal zones, all be out of work together?
DING:	That's always been my position, Doctor.
DR. B:	That's Democracy!
DING:	That's Show Business!
DR. B:	Well, Bill, you've been in some pretty tough races . . .
DING:	I've always been a racist and proud of it. A White Racist! I'm proud of the White Race — it gave me my start.

ONLY THE MANAGER APPLAUDS.

DR. B: Bill, tonight you're up against a tough act. It's not the first time you've been back to belly with some of the big ones, Bill, and they never spit back. How come?

DING: Money, Doctor. I was a wealthy man. I could hire anybody and therefore I was higher than anybody. Those days are gone forever. God saw fit to strike me down. Gone are the days when you could tell the cities by the color of their smoke. We had cold noses then. We were baked potatoes in the ovens of Progress. I'll never forget it — it was an Irishman, I think, who said . . .

DR. B: Save it for the Memoirs, Bill — who cares? What are you going to do for the folks tonight?

DING: Some legerdemain and feats of wizardry. I shall endeavor to deceive your senses with every turn of my hand, and confuse your minds with every slip of my finger.

DR. B: Just like the old days, hey, Mr. President? But can you capture this election? Can you beat the home-ton Duck from Cincinatti? Presenting — the Dazzling Ding, Doctor of Deception!

BILL DING DOES HIS LESS THAN DAZZLING MAGIC ACT, ENDING WITH HIS TRANSFORMATION INTO WOMAN.

APPLAUSE CUE

DR. B: Well, what's the verdict, Norman?

MANAGER: Well, here it is, Doctor. The Laff-o-Graff says 136!

DR. B: You lose, Mr. President! Our winner, the Dancing Duck from Cincinatti — Marlo Hortebagy!

APPLAUSE CUE

THE DOCTOR AND THE MANAGER DRESS MARLO UP AS THE WINNER AS A SINGER INTONES:

SINGER: There he is — He was unemployed!
Now he works — 9 to 5!
His Duck Act was unequaled! He's a winner at last!
Now his days of cheating on Welfare are past!
There he is — up from the dregs he is —
Walking on eggs he is —
Mr. Unemployed
(He keeps humming as the Manager speaks)

MANAGER: Marlo, you'll receive a one-way non-refundable non-transferable bus pass on one of the Flying Clippers of the Steubenville Municipal Bus Lines — the Now Way to Travel. While you're waiting for your high-priority job interview, you'll be put up with at the Lucky Spot Motel at 109th and Central on the East Side. You'll get free coffee every day while you wait — courtesy of Arco Vending Machines — the Quality Leader. Congratulations!!!

SINGER: There he is — he doesn't know where he is —
He's unaware he is — Mr. Unemployed!

AND OFF THEY ALL GO.

ASH GROVE ENCORE

Another piece from the mostly new November 1970 Ash Grove appearance, this Encore proffers a mid-term look at domestic politics.

ASH GROVE ENCORE

ANNOUNCER: Ladies and gentlemen. An important announcement. The Firesign Theatre proudly relinquishes its allotted encore time to a group in town this week only for a taping of the Andy Gump Show. From Moscow, Idaho — America's Most Beloved White Gospel Assembly — Col. Albert H. Psalter, leading his 16 Singing Men.

PSALTER (PP): Howdy, friends. I'm Col. Albert H. Psalter and we're happy to be here today. In fact, we're happy to be anywhere today — representing as we do, the Big Army of the Majority. Yes, we've been out among them — all over this country. Yes, we've been in a lot of tense situations — sometimes it was even hard for us to tell what tense we will be in — what tense we were in next. But — what am I talking about? We asked the people and they, of course, replied!

CHORUS: HAIRLIPED CROWD SOUNDS

PSALTER: Communication! That's what they wanted. Just listen to what they said . . .

CHORUS: HUMMMMMMM

VOICE 1 (DO): Life is not all that bad that we need something to break the reality of it.

CHORUS: HUMMMMMMM

VOICE 2 (PA): My husband is an oil-burner mechanic and he used to be on call 24 hours a day. No more. Now he doesn't work after dark. But then — what does?

CHORUS:	HUMMMMMMM
VOICE 3 (PB):	My Mother always used to say: "Think of the starving Chinese." Now we're all sorry we did.
PSALTER:	Yes, we're being pushed together like pigs. There *is* a sense of confusion! It's Electric! Questions are being asked faster than minds can be erased!
CHORUS:	HUMMMMMMM
VOICE 2:	What is reality?
CHORUS:	HUMMMMMMM
VOICE 3:	Why am I frightened all the time?
CHORUS:	HUMMMMMMM
VOICE 1:	Put your hands up!
CHORUS:	HUMMMMMMM
PSALTER:	Yes, exactly. What is reality? You won't find it by going into your neighbor's house when he's asleep. I've been there, and I know. So look at it. Take a good look at it. And you figure it out. Then join with us in the Big March of the Majority!
CHORUS:	(SINGING TO "GOD BLESS AMERICA") Silent Majority, Step to the Front! Don't be quiet, Start a riot, Then go clean up your room and behave! Under beer cans, Smell the sweat glands, See the nightsticks over you-ooo— Silent Majority, Count me one too! Three! Four! Five! (FADING OUT) 2 — 3 — 4 — 5 2 — 3 — For . . . ("AGE OF AQUARIUS") We're the voices of the Silent Majority . . . The Silent Majori-teee!
PSALTER:	Don't worry about them Minorities —

VOICE 2:	They can take care of themselves —
VOICE 1:	There's so many of them.
VOICE 3:	But remember, there's a lot of us too.
PSALTER:	And, after all, isn't everybody happy?
VOICE 1:	Aren't we being taken — good care of?
VOICE 3:	Trust your leaders.
VOICE 2:	Listen to what they say. (RAZZBERRY!)
PSALTER:	Just sit back and relax.
VOICE 3:	You might learn something.
VOICE 1:	Liberty is almost within our grasp.
VOICE 2:	So let's get her before someone else does.
VOICE 3:	We have our women to think of.
PSALTER:	And they've been thinking of us too.
VOICE 1:	Yes, there's room enough for everyone.
VOICE 2:	Don't be afraid to speak out.
PSALTER:	America is listening.
VOICE 3:	You've got a piece of this country — put it back.
VOICE 1:	Make friends with democracy.
VOICE 2:	She has knees, just like everyone else.
PSALTER:	So join the lunacy!
VOICE 3:	Blast off!
VOICE 1:	Catch the Moon Fever.

VOICE 2:	Don't worry, while you're gone, we'll take care of everything —
PSALTER:	And everybody — because this is a time of sudden change.
VOICE 3:	And you don't want to be left behind.
VOICE 1:	So let's march forward together! Forward, into the Past!
CHORUS (SING):	Violence and lust outstanding, Censorship and busts abounding. We will do our best to speak out — And the rest of us will sneak out — And a few of you will freak out! (MOMENT OF MINDLESS BABBLE) And the news will surely leak out That the world is — o — ver! We're — in — clover! 'Cause — There's room enough for all of us, If you'll please just step aside! There's room enough for all of us, If you'll swallow your silly pride (Go get a haircut!) If you can develop a rhinosaurus hide, Then tramp across the country — Far and wide — And you'll see That there's room enough for all of US! So won't you come along for the r-i-i-i-de! Won't you come along for, Why don't you come along for (Exact change please!) So won't you come along for the r-i-i-i-de!!
PSALTER:	Good night everybody. Have a Merry Juana and a Hashish New Year!

GIANT FLASH FEARED

CONFIDENTIAL

ROCKETS LOSE AGAIN

STUDIO CITY JUNE 29 (UPPER)

There were tears of joy and a cry of happiness in Mixville again last Monday, as the tie-and-die Mixville horsehide squad broke their hard-luck jinx and underpowered their opponents from Warner's 10-12, sending them into the cellar for the second time for this season.

It was the first time that the new Rocket swatmen worked together like a real team, although they had a scare given them in the sixth and seventh innings when Mixville pushed across six runs to go out front 10-8.

STORYBOOK FINISH

A small gathering of about 75 Persian fans began to leave the stands as apparent victory for Mixville was in sight for the hard-fighting Rockets. First, Murphy went down swimming, followed by Berkman flying out.

Two down and one out to go. First baseman Kornspan came to bat and ran the count to 3-2 before sketching a walk. As Kornspan lumbered down to first, a "flicker of hope" was still burning in the hearts of the Mixville minds. The "Man" came up next and sung late, sending a solid smash into right field that went all the way for a home room.   (Cont. on p. 2)

When interviewed by "Rocket" Managing Editor Andrew "The Pig" Lungitt, longtime Mixville resident John Light was asked what he feared most.

"A giant flash flood!" he replied.

DOPE RING SMASHED

By R. Correspondent

On Tuesday last, the "Rocket" office was besieged with complaints of "Strange Portents" in the skies above Mixville. Indeed, musings were heard from as far as Muscatine, Iowa, and Edendale, California. This reporter, fearing the heavens to be about to go "crack and tremble wide," as the ancients would have us believe, and being fleet of foot and awake, betook himself first to the hallowed door of Mixville's chief public servent, Mayor E. B. "Bud" Bolingbroke.

MAYOR STONED

"It's d*p*!" cried "Bud", springing from a semi-recumbent position, having been informed of comets crumbling in the heavens overhead, "And it is coming from somewhere around here! The Mayor went onto explain patiently to this somewhat startled, but by now semi-recumbent reporter, that citizen complaints in Mixville were at an all time low. Indeed, criminal sources said d*p* itself was at an all-time low and criminal complaints were out-
(Cont. on p. 2)

THE MIXVILLE "ROCKET"   VOL. I, NO. I   PAGE TWO

SPQRTS

Continued from p. I

KALLOSTIAN SPARKLES

The score was tied 10-10 and Mixville was back in the ballgame in their bitter fight to get into the pits. The winning run was on third with two outs.

DISASTER STRIKES

Then it happened. It all started with two straight singles off Berman, a walk and a triple to center, which cleaned the bases and makes the score 11-10. Disaster struck in the moment that followed.

SPORTS QUIZZED

1. At Boston, where on April 14, the Red Sox vs. Washington opener was delayed by a freaie snow storm that blanked Edendale?

BOX   SCORE   FRIDAY

FLOOD

Continued from p. I

distancing citizen complaints. "I don't want to insulate that there is more criminals in Mexviled than honest citizens," the late Mayor exhumed "but I'll bet money that's the case." "Lucky there's no d*p* around here or we'd have a situation on our hand" he brenfleed.

NO D*PE IN MIXVILLE

The "Rocket" fears it is in our neighboring "community" of Atwater.
Atwater people are different than Mixville people.

THE
MIXVILLE
"ROCKET"

Founded to Serve Mixville, "The Something Capitol of the World," and the surrounding communities of Edendale, Ivanhoe, Elysian Heights, Frogtown, Dogtown and Toonerville.

DECLARATION OF PRINCIPALS

"I'll provide the people of this city with a daily paper that will tell all the news honestly. I will also provide them with a fighting and tireless champion of their rights as citizens and human beings."

C. F. Dudley, Editor

FIRESIGN SACKED

MIXVILLE JULY 14 (DOWNER)

The Firesign Theatre, Amerika's beloved underground comedians, was fired today from their beloved underground avant-garde religious-type radio program.

"Today," Pogrom Director Les "Mr. Jazz" Carter said.

NO REASON

"Why were we fired," they said. No reason was given, as usual. Retiring with the Firesign Four is the beloved underground engineer, Lance Pvt. Vaugn The Live Earl Jive Philkins. Turn off your radio until further notice.

THE MIXVILLE "ROCKET"   PAGE FOUR

LOCALIZIN' WITH THE "ROCKET"

TOURING TIPS

MIXVILLE
A Community Divided By Itself. Motto: Look out for that great big bird!" Home of the Tom Mix Movie Ranch.

Romantic EDENDALE
"The City That God Forgot." Home of the Mack Sennett and Selig Film Studios.

Doughty Little IVANHOE
"Foursquare Upon The Northern Line." Home of the 1st. Semi-Annual Hyperion Bridge Championships.

ELYSIAN HEIGHTS
"Overlooking Everything, and Remembering Nothing." A respectable residential community.

SHOPPING WITH THE "ROCKET"

When in downtown Mixville, your Editor suggests you eat at THE PIZZA PALACE for good pizza, imported beer and ask for Flash Gordon. Laundry done easy at *SILVER STAR* CLEANERS, and SILVERGLEN LIQUORS sells the "Free" Press.

And be sure and visit Irv's SHERWOOD FOREST for a night on-the-town in Ivanhoe. You can count on clean beer and wholesome entertainment -- Mother, popcorn and pool.

Down on the Sunset Strip in Edendale, wise guys will be in for wise buys, when they shop at MINETTE'S ANTIQUES AND ETC. And don't forget METAMORPHOSIS, THE BURRITO KING and Art at ART'S PHOTO

MORE FOR YOU IN ISSUE #2!!!

The "Rocket" welcomes newstips and stories. Leave at Metamorphosis with Cappy.

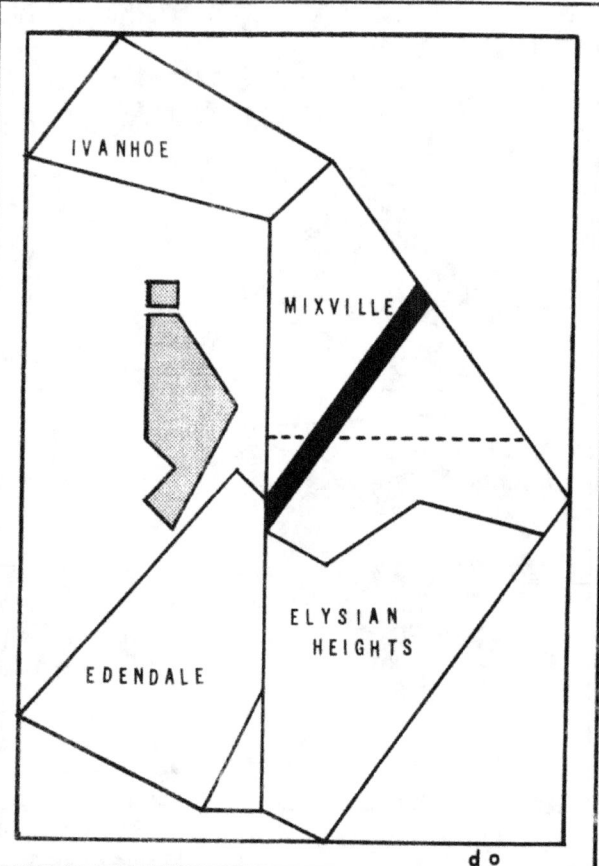

SOLID JACKSON!

Mixville's own boogie band is currently playing. At the Brass Ring on Ventura Blvd. in Sherman's Oaks. They'll beat you, daddy-O, eight to the bar, every night except Monday. Solid, Jackson!

MIXVILLE ROCKETS!

Mixville's own boogie softball team meets every Monday at 6 p.m. for practice. Look for the $1,000,000 outfield in tie-die at the Elysian Fields.

THE BOB SIDEBURN NEWS

Written by The Firesign Theatre and performed at the Ash Grove, November 1970. It was performed for the television program "About A Week" in March 1971.

ORIGINAL CAST
Phil Austin as Bob Sideburn, Walter, Alvarado

Peter Bergman as Hole Earth Estates Announcer, Ernie Mopa, Jim Naseum, Local Announcer, Spud

David Ossman as Og Oggilby, Don G. O'Vanni, Happy Kornspan, Darlene Yuckamoto

Phil Proctor as Mickey West, Tenor, Bill Sailor, Pico

THE BOB SIDEBURN NEWS

ANNOUNCER: It's 9 P.M., curfew time. Children — do you know who your parents are?

MUSIC: THEME

ANNOUNCER: The BOB SIDEBURN NEWS! With University-trained analyst, Dr. Og Oggilby O.G., Big Jim Naseum with Servo-Sports, and Bill Sailor in the weather balloon. And now, here's NOW, with the Tri-City's newest NOW-caster — BOB SIDEBURN!

BOB: Good evening. Well, the Governor's Garbage Moratorium bill took a fall today down the back stairs of the House, but the old man bounced back like a rubber weasel. In the aftermath of guerilla attacks on child care centers, the city council asks for stiffer animal regulation controls — and — plague of troll victims under bridges levels off. All this and more, plus dogs, darkies and Darlene, after this interesting time out...

SOUND FX: BIRDS, WIND, HARMONICA

VOICE: Birds...wind...bunnies...trees...water...peace... The hallmarks of natural living — once available only to animals and the very rich, now it can be yours — thanks to the Frank S. Hutton Company. HOLE EARTH ESTATES — ecologically controlled for your precious health and safety. Traditional Frank S. Hutton features include: Guarded landfill, thousands of acres of primeval forest available to you on closed-circuit TV, and miles of winding, roomy storm drains for your high-speed fishing and boating pleasure. Take the

Lenore Hutton turnoff, off the New Democratic Freeway, to HOLE EARTH ESTATES — the ultimate in the illusion of privacy!

BOB: Of course, first in the heart of everyone's mind — the election. It's page one, it's what's happening, it's Now — it's all over. Why? Professor Og Oggilby, what's the nitty gritty?

OG: Well, Bob, an off-year political thunderstorm split Joe Voter down the middle last night, and all the clenched houses and all the old men couldn't get it together again. And tonight, that looks like that means never — and that's a long, long time. You were probably watch-dogging along with everyone else at about 9:01 City Time, when even the computers threw up their hands and, fed up, read out: "What's happening?" Let's play it back, the way it happened, just the way it was...

WEST: ...ickey West, here at the Universal Ballroom of the Downtown Atomic Hotel, Downtown, where, for a few brief hours, this is where it's at. We're all here, waiting for the fireworks to go off. This giant room is packed with reporters, newsmen and journalists, and members of the press. I see a lot of faces here that I've seen before. And they're all waiting, and we're waiting. What we're all waiting for is, literally, something to happen. It's been quiet here most of the evening, but that's understandable because nothing has happened yet. It's too early to say what, if anything, is going on now. Or, what we can expect in the future — if anything. Most of the candidates' younger members are left on the floor — there's a group of three- or four-year-old children playing over there in a corner of the room — they're playing piñata with one of the little girls. A mood of undisturbed quiet prevails right now — the band is on a break, and several men behind me have sat down. Here's one of them now — a familiar if virtually unknown power behind the scenes — let me get through here — Ernest Mopa? Ern? Ern, do we have a minute here?

MOPA: What time is it?

WEST:	Ha, ha. Ernie, you've got one foot in the back — what's going on at this stage?
MOPA:	On stage? Nothing now — the band's eating...
WEST:	No — I mean...
MOPA:	You mean — ?
WEST:	I mean right here.
MOPA:	Right here? Well, it ought to be pretty clear to everybody by now that everything that's happening isn't here. It's happening behind the scenes.
WEST:	Of course...and you ought to know.
MOPA:	Yes, I should, I really should. Behind the scenes. You know what I mean.
WEST:	Yes, you should. So maybe you can tell us. What's really happening?
MOPA:	Well, in terms of development, basically nothing. However, what no one ever realizes in these situations is that the groundwork that we got laid — or that has been laid behind the scenes — is completed. Now, it's just a matter of waiting — to see what's going to happen...if anything at all.
WEST:	— er — How long do you think we'll have to wait?
MOPA:	At this stage?
WEST:	Well, backstage.
WALTER (FILTER):	Mickey...Mickey, this is Walter.
WEST:	Walter!?
WALTER:	Yes, it's Walter.
MOPA:	Is that Walter?

WALTER: Yes, it is, Mr. Mopa. All of us here couldn't help but wonder if there was something that you said that you didn't tell us.

MOPA: Well, Walter, I can only speak for myself — and my associates — our position is that while nothing has happened yet — still, before all the sound and fury, nothing significant can happen — to signify anything...

WEST: That's right, Walter.

INTERMITTENT DROPOUTS BEGIN TO CREEP INTO THE CONVERSATION

WALTER: Then we ...ight be ...orrect in our assumption here, that — up to now — ...othing's happening...

WEST: What did you say, Walter?

MOPA: Is that Walter? It doesn't sound like Walter.

THE TRANSMISSION BREAKS UP — AD LIB

OG: That was the way it started, but it couldn't go on like that forever. Had only three people voted, the results would have been the same. And I may be using a 9-iron when I need a putter, but that's Democracy. And it may be old-fashioned to say I'm proud of it, but, by golly — it scares hell out of me. Bob?

BOB: You've got a mouthful, Og. In other news, Mrs. Daisy Singleton, white, female, 35, of the Eastside Community Freeway Reclamation Project, stated at closing ceremonies for 26 miles of the New Democratic Freeway this afternoon that 23 miles will go under the plow Monday, principally in soya beans, peanuts and other pleasure crops. The remaining three miles? Well — tennis, anyone? Big Jim Naseum up next after this word to the wise and his wifes...

TENOR: ITALIAN DRINKING SONG

DON:	You all recognize the Saloon Song from "The Floating Prince" by Stein — now, here's the lilting Revenge Duet from "Il Vino Confuso"...
SINGERS:	DUELLING SCENE
DON:	Isn't that beautiful? It's by a great Italian composer. He's dead now, but lives on, in steerio hi-fi, on this 12-inch record album of 40 Great Unclaimed Melodies. If you were to go into a record store and ask for them, they'd think you were crazy. Hello, I'm Don G. O'Vanni, and I'm proud to speak for the Musical Heritage Surplus Club of Hong Kong. Wouldn't you like to raise the level of your home? Bring your family closer together around the hi-fi, listening to such immortal pieces of art, like Bidet's "The Fountain", or The Duke's Duet from "Il Schizophreno"? And if you act now, we'll include at absolutely no cost to anyone, this collection of 40 Familiar Sound Effects. Who can forget...
SOUND:	CAR START
DON:	...and...
SOUND:	CAR SKID AND CRASH
DON:	Remember...
SOUND:	WHISTLE
DON:	...and...
SOUND:	EXPLOSION
DON:	Well, they're all yours. And, if you act in time, we'll throw in this three-record boxed bonanza of Timeless Big Band Hymns. Titles like "In a Persian Melon", "Marching to Shibboleth", "My Spanish Suitcase", "The Happy Plunderer", "Waltz for Three People", and "The Hawaiian Hallucination Song". A cultural landslide to fill your home entertainment center. Write now — to this address...

TENOR: RUSSIAN SONG UNDER

LOCAL ANNOUNCER: Write MUSIC DEAL, box four-one-five, (SILENCE) — remember that's MUSIC DEAL, box four-one-five, (SILENCE)

BOB: Well, the computers finally reached a common cord today in Zurich. Big Bobby IV and Druzhba 6 chattered over the Blue Line for the first time since the European dislocation. And the result? A programmed agreement to keep out of each other's memory banks. What does this mean? Well, first of all, Mrs. Housewife will see the return of those exotic foods to her pantry — Mr. Cocktail can "get it on" again with a double chocolate vodka — and Little Miss Bobby Soxer will be bugging you for a credit writeoff at the local Soviet Boutique. Of course, every silver lining has a dark cloud. With that story — Eric Fudd in Zurich...

ERIC: The Salzburg Accord means the immediate dismemberment of GORBODUC — the intercontinental revenge network — one of the largest employers left on both sides of the Big Ditch. This will be a tremendous blow to many, if not most, of the crack job holders left. What are they going to do? This is Elmer Zurich...Salzburg...Fudd.

BOB: Of course the big layoffs don't affect any of us here in the entertainment industry, Og.

OG: Or in the world of good sports, Bob.

BOB: That's right! And here's the best sport we've got. Here's Big Jim Naseum...

JIM: Thanks, Bob Sideburn. Well, the Russians and the Americans may be shaking circuits in Salzburg, but it was all shake, rattle and roll down on the electric green turbo-turf at the Luna-Drome last night, when the San Francisco Cyborgs mashed memory banks with the Stalingrad Steelheads. It was Mecco-Football at its roughest, its toughest, and its most gruelingly technical. There was no score at the beginning — ha — but by the end of the first quarter, the Cyborgs had their first taste of oil. The Rooskies' crowd-pleasing robot Ivan the Technical, personally programmed by Servo-Coach Hilo Watanabe, used its fine new reasoning capacity to lead the Steelheaders to a 14 to 16 victory over San Francisco. In picnics today, the Central Park Lunchpails over-ate the Griffith Park Hampers 5 to 4, and — when the smoke cleared, it was Yosemite Cookouts 3, the Woodburners of Woodstock 6, in a doubleheader on California grass Saturday. Going local, there's a great card at the SuperDump tonight — game promoter Happy Kornspan must have gone crash-crazy, because he's lined up a matched set of beefy Stromberg-Carlson TVs to face a mixed team of kitchen appliances from Bakersfield. We spoke with Happy at the Dump this afternoon...

HAPPY: Well, Jim — yer right about the tremendous amount of destruction we're going to see tonight. Now, you take one of yer typical Ivan the Technical servo-mechs — now, they're only good fer a couple of games. By the time they come down here, they got no left or right capability — no oblique — just fast forward. So when we slap one on the back of one of them big glass water heaters and send it off hopping down the field, we just hope it's a match for the powerful chassis and the pure entertainment value of one of those Strombergs.

JIM: And that's all I wrote for Mecco-Sports tonight. I'm James Naseum. Catch my action on Adult Sports at 11.

BOB: Hope that's all you catch, Jim! Well, 800-odd residents of the sleepy tourist town of Hollywood, California, get a surprise in their mailbags today — anonymous form letters from the Government assuring them that their arrests for marijuana possession, backed up in the courts for as much as 40 years in some cases, have been forgotten. Officially. And speaking of highs, here, with the lowdown on the weather, Bill Sailor...

BILL: Thanks, Bob — the less we speak about *my* highs this weekend, the better. But I was out again today and temperatures felt normal to me — generally hovering around 98.6 — and the winds — well, you don't need a weatherman to tell which way the wind blows! Now, if we take a look at the weather picture this weekend, you'll find that when Weatherman II passed over our town today, it sent down this remarkably clear view of the stratospheric conditions over the whole continent, and then it burned up over Mexicali. Up here, around the Great Lakes — well, this negative seems to be reversed, so...down here around the Little Lakes, a well-developed low — well, actually, that's probably a high — appears to be influencing the reports of strong winds in the Southwestern Plains area. Looking over to the far West, which is of course the far East on your map, you see here a detailed feedback image, caused by ionospheric projection, or in layman's terms, an electrical ...ick...ip. The face may seem familiar to some of you older folks — can any of you guess who it is? Yes — it's Lt. Dan Matthews of "Highway Patrol" — the young Broderick Crawford. A great profile, but he's unfortunately blotted out all the weather from Portland right on up to San Diego. Nothing really new, but it's a happy change from those "I Married Joan" episodes that have been plaguing Western weathermen for weeks. There seems to be no end to electronic pollution in sight, since we are just now beginning to pick up bounce-back emissions from the late 1950s. How does it happen? No one knows for sure. But it looks like soon Weathermen will have to start looking up at the weather instead of looking down on it! And for somebody like me who spends most of his time up there in a balloon, that can be a pretty sad state of affairs... There is some hope, of course, that the newly deployed moon station, the SAMWPA — Spiro Agnew Memorial Weather Picture Antenna — will begin to send us clearer, or at least cleared, pictures from the surface of our oldest satellite. But so far the only valid information we've received has been weather reports from the moon...which continues to be sunny and warm, with temperatures ranging from the low- to mid-200s... Well, locally — reception will be fair to hazy, with little or no snow...and those conditions will continue until early tomorrow morning. And folks, the frost warnings are up — so remember to turn your electric blankets back a full hour before you get up. As for tomorrow's weather — well, we'll just have to wait until tomorrow. 10-4! Bob?

BOB: 21-50 bye, Bill. The locusts came back in swarms over Pomona today, signaling the historic beginning of the Feast of the Inaccurate Contraception. For the faithful of this sleepy little spa nestled in the foot of the California hardhills, this means the annual Running of the Chickens — an event made a part of our Now way of life by being written about in books by famous authors. With a holiday report, here's Darlene Yuckamoto...

DARLENE: I'm here at the Our Mother of the Greyhound Bus Station Plaza in sultry Pomona, waiting, like everyone else, for the thrilling event which culminates this fabulous and exciting day of flatulence and heavy drinking. Of course, who knows more about El Running de los Chickens, than famous author Spud Fowler. You're more than an offer — author, though, Mr. Fowler, you're an aficionado of this dangerous sport. Can you explain the complicated procedure that visitors will see tomorrow?

SPUD: At dusk, Darlene, the Plaza will resound with the sound of the LA POLOMBRA, or "red egg" being nailed to the back door of the church. Then, the BRUJAS or "old ladies" with their BRUHAHAS — literally, "cock-teasers" or "chicken brooms" — enrage the chickens by awakening them and pushing them down the street. In only a few short hours, the spontaneous honking of taxi-cab horns signals the rounding of the first turn. Then the young men, crouched in the shadows of LA CANTINA, know that only a few short hours remain before LOS BOUNCEROS or bar-sweeps push the young men out onto the sidewalk. And there they must face their hour or hour and a half of truth. I come to watch it every year. The sense of desperate confusion puts hair on my palms.

DARLENE: And here are two of the brave young CHICALONES who will go out to challenge fate in the middle of the night. Why, if I may ask, do you do it?

PICO: To become a man!

SPUD: Isn't that beautiful?

ALVARADO: So nobody can call you chicken!

DARLENE: Don't you young men ever think about the danger?

PICO: Yeah.

ALVARADO: No.

PICO: We only live for the moment.

ALVARADO: Yeah! What time is it?

DARLENE: You've survived more than one of these fiascos, Mr. Pico. What was the most exciting thing that ever happened to you?

ALVARADO: Who's excited?

PICO: ...ah...every year is as exciting as the next, and when those big POLLONES, those sweaty chickens come around the corner, lost & angry — the heat is terrible —

ALVARADO: Yeah, the ones in heat are the most terrible! They got a family to protect...

PICO: And then, at that bery moment, when I know for chure that within the next fifteen minutes I'm going to have to face them — a thrill of reverence and sheer disgust runs down my leg.

ALVARADO: Yeah. They're looking for a place to nest.

PICO: That's called the ENCOMBRA — and, lady, you better not be under them when they do it... (MUTTERS IN SPANISH)

ALVARADO: Yucky!

DARLENE: How thrilling, yet sad somehow.

ALVARADO:	Yeah...?
SOUND FX:	WHISTLE
PICO:	That's the whistle.
DARLENE:	What does it mean?
ALVARADO:	It's twelve o'clock.
PICO:	Time for lunch.
DARLENE:	You must be starving. What are you having?
ALVARADO:	Chicken-fried beer. May the fiasco continue! See you at the bar, baby!
PICO:	(SINGS, TO "LA CUCARACHA") Las pollones! Las pollones! No me gusta encontrar / Las pollones! Las pollones! You can find us in the bar...
DARLENE:	And so, the fiasco continues, on and on through the long, hot summer day. Spowler Fudd put it best, I think, when he wrote in his 20th Century classic A CHICKEN IN THE STREET — "God, how he loved those chickens. Those chickens were the best things he'd seen since he left home. Left home to stand here on and on through the long, hot summer day, wearing his steel hat. The sun never sets when you're wearing a steel hat, he thought, proudly." Darlene Yuckamoto, KFST News, Pomona.
BOB:	Thanks Darlene — Og, Bill, Jim — we'll be back with our shirts off at 11. It's been all the news, all the time. Stay tuned for the insane movie — "Two Guys and a Goat." The flag flies high tonight over the U.S. Government — where it belongs! This is Bob Sideburn — keep swinging — goodnight.

THE MARTIAN SPACE PARTY

Presented 8:30 to 10:00 p.m. on March 30, 1972 live in Strange Hall at KPFK-FM, Cahuenga Boulevard, North Hollywood. The broadcast performance was recorded by a Columbia Records crew and filmed by a team led by Steve Gillmor and Bill McIntyre, who co-produced both the broadcast and film.

Between November 11, 1971 and February 24, 1972, Firesign presented twelve episodes of "Let's Eat!," an hour-long mostly weekly show on KPFK. "The Martian Space Party" liberated material and characters contributed in script form or by improvisation to "Let's Eat!" by the individual members of the group and imbedded them in the headlines of the moment — Nixon on his way to China and the coming Presidential election — in a countdown both for the launch and the nomination, with a Japanese Movie Monster wreaking havoc on both.

The writing began on February 15, with the opening of the Surrealist Party Convention. (Four years later the team of Papoon and Tirebiter, with their slogan of "Not Insane!" had a nation-wide "Campoon.") The two scenes for "Anythynge You Want To" were written for the MSP, joining the slowly evolving script. "Young Guy, Motor Detective" added to the Japanese subtext. A number of new songs were featured in the so-Seventies Space Bubble Cabaret, thanks to the frequent introduction of original music on "Let's Eat!"

THE MARTIAN SPACE PARTY

SCENE: A CLEARING IN SPACE

KPFK ANNOUNCER: . . . And now KPFK presents The Firesign Theatre's Martian Space Party!

CUE APPLAUSE. GAVEL RAPS.

SPEAKER FUDD (PB): The Convention of the National Surrealist Light People's Party — not affiliated with the National Surrealist School of Broadcasting — will please come to order! My fellow delegates!

GAVEL RAPS. AUDIENCE REPONDS AS ANIMALS.

SPEAKER: Chairwoman Furberger, steamed colleagues and stewed members of the press! Will the National Spider Caucus *please* scuttle back to your seats — it's nice to have you, but you're making some of the flies nervous. And now, I'd like to introduce, if I may . . . excuse me . . .

WORKER BRINGS IN A NOTE. SOTTO VOCE CONVERSATION.

WORKER (PP): There's a human-sized, bottle-green convertible blocking the entrance to the California Rats valet parking lot. And your lights are on. Thank you.

SPEAKER: Now, if you please, I'd like to introduce the first Guest Chaplin for tonight's opening session. Let's welcome him as if he wasn't what he is — a Man of God — the Mighty Video Vicar — Rev. Bob Tackle!

CUE APPLAUSE

BOB (DO): I'm mighty pleased to be here, Speaker Fudd. It's always a pleasure for a prophet to come here to San Clamaron, a wonderful resort town on beautiful Gas War Island. Now, Dear Friends . . .

ORGAN MUSIC UNDER

BOB: You know, fans, this is just the beginning of God's exciting game, and what happens now? What happens when you're shaking inside to go wide? When you go out on a pattern and get overthrown? When it's man-to-man defense and you anticipate the snap? What a rush! Look out! Another quick penalty, another personal foul! An elbow was caught and you see it! Is it sudden death — or sudden victory? Well, Dear Friends, as we take care of our National business here tonight, you know He's watching with you. Remember, He's the Number One Fan, and whatever happens, He's enjoying it, because He's Top Dog, and not the other way around. There's no score yet. It's your football, friends — don't lose possession!

CUE APPLAUSE AND ANIMAL NOISES.

BOB: Now, let me introduce, direct from the Convenient Karate Baptist Chapel of the Bulls, my own Martian Minstrels — the New Space Dixie Choraleers!

CUE APPLAUSE. ORGAN CONTINUES.

CHORALEERS: Oh, Blinding Light, O light that blinds,
I cannot, cannot see!
The sun's behind the moon's bright shine —
Who will look out for me?
Look out! Look out! That space-hole tube
To see the Eye of God!
You know for sure He's watching you
His lonely, only job!

BOB: That was beautiful! Now, let's all join voices ...

TINY STEPS SUDDENLY ON MIKE AND PULLS OUT A SMALL SIGN WHICH READS "STOP KILLING SPIDERS!"

TINY: My fellow delegates. Except for the snakes. If God were registered, I'm sure He'd vote the same way I'm going to. Or maybe not. Well, anyway — Stop eating each other! Not Insane!

THE AUDIENCE RESPONDS "NOT INSANE!"

SPEAKER: Come to order! This is entirely improvised! None of this was written down! The entertainment will continue just as soon as the snakes return to their sacks or baskets! Please!

THE POINT-OF-VIEW TURNS FROM THE CONVENTION TO THE NETWORK COMMENTATORS.

WALTER (PP): Well, apparently the entertainment will continue from the floor of the National Surrealist Light People's Party Convention, under the newly completed Rotodrome, there in San Clamaron. And did you see what that girl was holding up there on our monitor, Walter?

WALTER (PA): Yes. No. Apparently not, Walter. I was plugged into the feed from Monster Island, where the President has just been refused entrance again to the Forbidden City.

WALTER: Well, you know, Walter, it is one of the most popular rides on the Island. What I saw was ... well, I'm getting a report on it now ... Apparently she held up a picture of the back-end of a baboon! Well, that's certainly the most controversial thing we've seen so far.

WALTER: And yet apparently the most interesting.

WALTER: Yes. That's true, wouldn't you agree, Walter?

WALTER: I don't know. I wasn't listening.

WALTER: We'll be back to our live coverage of both the Surrealist Convention and the Embarkation of the President's Martian Space Party, after these important simulated announcements . . .

PB AND DO, BACK TO BACK, ON THE TELEPHONE

PEORGE: Well, gollee, Veronica! I don't think I'm obnoxious.

VERONICA: Well that's the way I felt at the slumber party, and everybody agreed.

PEORGE: You mean you called me all the way long distance just to humiliate me? Whose credit card are you using?

VERONICA: Hubert Humphrey's.

ANNOUNCER (PP): Yes, no matter where you are, we'll find you and plug you in, to somewhere where something is happening. And even if it's unpleasant, you're paying for it. In the air, in the car, or in your bed — could we listen to what you've said? This message was brought to you by your local National Phone Company — a part of Inter-Ach — the International Division of Arachnid Industries.

BACK TO THE NETWORK GUYS.

WALTER (PA): While the President recovers from that stunning rejection on Monster Island, and before things get hot down on San Clamaron, Eric? Eric?

ERIC (DO): Yes?

WALTER: I'd like to ask you a question. How are things on Monster Island?

ERIC: Well, as we've seen here all this past week, there's so much noise here — and it's made the President cry — and there are so many other things that make the President cry as well — the steam, the unforgettable smells, and the unpleasant religious overtones for an emotional Christian like the President, all these have contributed to a confusing — even senseless — sense of senseless confusion and chaos.

WALTER: Tell me again about the Monsters, Eric.

ERIC: It's not so much the Monsters, Walter, as the dreadful fear and senseless destruction. Anyone can see the President just doesn't know what to do with his hands . . .

WALTER: Pardon me, Eric, but we've been told that we're to return to the floor of the Convention now, where General D. C. Blame of the Veteran's Tap-Dance Administration is . . . has already begun his address to the sleeping delegates . . .

RETURNING TO THE CONVENTION PODIUM

GENERAL (PP): . . . the toilet was hopelessly clogged and both our parachutes were still at the cleaners. What's that? I said, pointing to a clearing ahead. My co-pilot, God, replied: "That's the Burma oil fields." Well, hell, I said. Don't the Japs get fuel from there? "Sure," said God, "everybody knows that." Well, then, I said, let's drop our bombs on 'em, turn the hell around and get back to base! Well, God looked at me and said: "Colonel, you fool, sir — we can't do that!" And why the hell not? I asked. "Because," he said, "those oilfields are owned by the British — and they're our allies!" Well, then, what the hell're they doin' givin' fuel to the enemy? I said. "Well, Colonel," He said, "I guess they need the income to help us fight the war!" Well, sir, we had a good laugh over that one, dropped our load on a herd of sacred cows near Fiji, and belly-flopped in the ocean. It was a good landing, but God was killed, and of course, I survived and floated to shore using His body as ballast! I tell you, that was one of the wildest theatres of war I ever played in . . . But that's not to say I've stopped fighting! Just because

| | the war might soon be over doesn't mean we have to stop. There must be a good cause somewhere and we can find it if anybody can. We now occupy this great hall, agitated and confused as we are, it's my fervent hope that we might please stop eating each other long enough to nominate some man . . . |

BOOS AND ANIMAL NOISES FROM THE AUDIENCE.

GENERAL: Or some — anything. Any one of you! So let's get down to it, down to business now, before . . . Damn!

PB BRINGS IN ANOTHER NOTE.

WORKER (PB): 'Scuse me, I have a message here . . . is there a delegation of rats caucusing in the air conditioning system? If so, will you please, if you can hear me, please contact the Credentials Committee for your proper room assignments!

THE GENERAL AND THE WORKER TAKE A MINUTE TO SPEAK OFF-MIKE AND THE SCENE RETURNS TO THE NETWORK.

ERIC: Walter?

WALTER (PA): I couldn't hear you, Eric, but it does now seem that we'll soon be re-establishing contact with Charles B. Smith at the Forbidden City at Monster Island, where, presumably the President has finally stopped crying and is preparing himself for the evening launch attempt.

ERIC: We'll go out to launch, or whatever happens, and now, here's more from the Convention floor, where . . . oh . . . after   . . . oh . . . this . . .

THIS IS A REALLY CHEAP COMMERCIAL.

ANN ONE: "I Was Hitler's Dog Doctor! By Dr. Lt. Fritz Kraut!

ANN TWO: Yes! It's available to you in a personal, rubber-bound edition.

ANN THREE:	Now, and for the first time! The Schnifter's whole incredible private life as revealed for lots of money by his trusted personal physician and psychiatrist, Dr. Lt. Fritz Kraut! An ex-Nazi, writing with medical-college frankness and making the most sensational disclosures ever made about any person!
ANN FOUR:	Talk about rotten physiological backgrounds! These terrible confessions! These ghastly self-revelations! If you hate Hitler now — no word yet invented will describe your feelings after you have read . . .
ONE & TWO:	"I Was Hitler's Dog Doctor!"
ANN THREE:	Yes! Through fifteen boring years this mad fiend poured out his psychoanalitical sickness in startling man-to-man conversations with Dr. Lt. Kraut! Indeed, most of these authenticated revelations are so affecting, they may not even be mentioned and had to be deleted from the book!
ANN ONE:	Now, you too!! For only one dollar and 29 cents, can know as much about Der Schnifter as does Dr. Lt. Kraut! You must read this book!!
ANN TWO:	Rush at me with my copy! When the policeman arrives at my door, I will pay him a dollar-29, plus small postage and DOA charges. I understood that I must read the book in his presence, and if not entirely satisfied, he will return me to you at once, no questions asked, and at No Additional Cost!!
ANN FOUR:	You must not miss this fantastic offer!
ANN THREE:	Hurry!!!!
ANN ONE:	Before the War ends!

THE ANNOUNCERS SNAP TO A SALUTE AND THE PARTY TAKES A MUSIC BREAK WITH HELEN KANE'S "HE'S SO UNUSUAL."

THE CONVENTION RESUMES FROM THE PODIUM.

SPEAKER FUDD: . . . 'nd many years ago, fellow delegates, a very simple man — a horse-waterer from Indiana — wrote down some words that has meant more to every succeeding generations of young Americans than the last. The writer, of course, was the great philatelist himself, Charles Everett Fellatio. His famous poem, "I Am The President's Man," will now be read by the famous and beloved Philippino character actor, Sir Charles Gangabangalang. Sir Charles . . .

CUE APPLAUSE. ORGAN MUSIC PLAYS UNDER:

CHARLES: I am the President's man.
I like what the President likes.
If the President likes the Dodgers,
I like the Dodgers.
When the President stands up in the cold at Valley Forge, I stand up beside him.
If the President has blue cheese dressing and the baked potato, can I be different?
Yes, I am the President's Man. If the President sits on a stump, I'd be proud to sit on that stump just behind him.
At Montenegro Bay . . . At Dorkas Point . . . In the Philippine War . . . At Bum's Spit . . . He was there . . .
At Rudy's . . . At the Ritz . . . At 21 . . . Dancing all night . . . He was there . . .
And I was right behind him . . . like a bridge.
Sour cream and chives on your baked potato?
Yes, ma'm . . . Just like the President.

ORGAN MUSIC SWELLS AND FADES OUT.

SPEAKER: That's beautiful. Beautiful words. Words our uncles and mothers hung in their windows as they went forward behind the President, leveling mountains and filling valleys. Until that day. That fatal night!

DOCUMENTARIAN (DO): This is a real document, written by a real American high school student who was really there the day after The Day He Died. You were listening on your radios or watching on one of the 140 television sets that existed then; but he, like forty-three other finalists in the National Spelling Bee, were actually there on the sidewalk between two federal buildings next to a crowd of Negro train engineers who had stopped their trains that day to say goodbye to an era. His name was William Spraeckeler — a name harder to spell than most of the hundred-odd-thousand he had memorized in the last year to get here. But even to a high school student it seemed strange — that his body was going to pass by on the very street where he had walked down to receive his oath of office.

NEGRO (PA); Hah!

DOC: One of the Negros whispered laughingly . . .

NEGRO: How Can A Dead Man Be President Of The United States?

DOC: Everybody laughed because they were so sad, and to the boy the laughter sounded like train whistles. An old woman across the street lifted up a bottle of gin and cried . . .

OLD WOMAN (PP): I've never taken a drink in my life, but, by God, he's dead now and I'm going to drink forever!

DOC: By now, real people were beginning to collect next to the fire-plug on the adjacent corner, shading their heads from the sun with giant newspaper headlines . . .

NEWS (PA): He's dead!

DOC TWO (PB): This is what the high school boy was seeing while his mind was remembering any time he could remember a picture of the great man. He could remember only a couple of pictures and the way his father said his name — very much like the way his fifth-grade teacher had said his name and he could think hard enough to feel that it was important;

	but he couldn't feel it the way he could feel his feet when he wriggled his toe or the way he could pretend to feel lots of other things.
DOC:	One Negro pointed a long rustling finger at an office building where the secretaries had hung their hair out the window in a show of grief. Everybody had seen a lot of that kind of emotion during the war, and today they were mourning the Great Man of Mourning. The high school boy cried because he was so sad . . .
DOC TWO:	The proud and the powerful cried because they had lost a Great Friend . . .
DOC:	The Germans and the Japanese cried because they had lost a Great Enemy and a Great War . . .
DOC TWO:	The poor cried because the liquor stores were closed.
REPORTER (PP):	No breeze . . . Every girl in Washington seems to go hatless, her hair hanging loose. I almost said flowing in the breeze, but there was no breeze this morning . . . The half-staffed flags everywhere hung limply against their poles. A man put up a stepladder up the street and, thus posted, had a fine view . . .
BOY (DO):	I loved his voice on the radio, father . . .
REPORTER:	The boy said . . .
BOY:	It always sounded so nice and friendly, even when I didn't understand all he was talking about. I loved the way he said, "My-ah, Frans . . . "
MAN (PA):	Yes . . .
REPORTER:	The man said . . .
MAN:	And I used to say that he was just a medicine man, selling his wares to the people with that seductive voice. What crazy things political hate will make a man say . . .

THE ORGAN MUSIC SWELLS AND WE RETURN TO THE CORRESPONDENTS.

WALTER (PP): The tribute to the Last Great Resident of The United States on Earth continues from the podium of the Light People's Surrealist Convention. And it appears that the President is now sleeping on Monster Island. Or, our correspondent is. Right, Walter?

WALTER (PA): What?

WALTER (PP): Perhaps this would be a good time to discuss some of the remarkable security arrangements — precautions — that allow the President to go to sleep anytime he wants to. Earlier today I spoke with the Senior Agent in Charge of his Operations, and we thought for a while that we'd lost the tape, but we've found it now, and it appears that it had merely been cleared — though security. Rather ironic, right, Walter? Eric?

ERIC (DO): Well, I've got a good idea, Walter — I've been instructed that now would be a good time to show that tape you did with the old cop this afternoon.

WALTER (PP): Well, alright. Let's see that tape . . . now . . .

THE "TAPE" BEGINS, THEN "REWINDS" AND BEGINS AGAIN.

WALTER ("ON TAPE"): . . . ith me in the studio now . . . oing to talk a bout . . . wonoidutsehtniemhtiwbrrp . . . Sitting with me in the studio now, and we're going to talk about it with him.

MR BLANK (PA): Yes, Mr. Announcer, everyone is hearing about espionage agents and saboteurs so much now it's hard to think . . . that just a few years ago, no one even knew that saboteurs had agents.

WALTER: Yes. To start off with, Mr. Blank, what are some of the violations handled by the Squad which are not as well known as the White Trash Traffic Act and the National Migratory Sponge Theft Act?

BLANK: Well, for example, you, Mr. Announcer, are presently in violation of the Concealed Radio Statute. Yes, by not broadcasting the call letters of this radio station every half hour you could be jeapordizing the security of this area and my family and friends within its perimeters.

WALTER: Gosh, Mr. Blank. This is exciting and serious as if it were real.

BLANK: Oh, of course this is real, and you'll be convicted and sent to Radio Prison.

WALTER: No doubt, Mr. Blank. Many of our viewers who have traveled around extensively — and other small towns in Arizona — will remember that Radio Prison is located in this particular section of extremely rugged and unusual beauty because of the Pointed Desert nearby and the many vari-colored canyons.

BLANK: Yes. Where the colored people are kept.

WALTER: Mr. Blank, though we think of women as the Gentile Sex, I recall that in the past you G-Men have been dealt from the bottom of the deck of sex with some who were not gentle in any sense of the term.

BLANK: That makes sense to me, Mr. Announcer. Yes, a Special Agent was once assigned the task of taking fifteen percent of a mannish, big-boned woman of 150 pounds who was charged with shooting a Frog.

WALTER: That must have been terrible, Mr. Blank.

BLANK: Yes, Mr. Announcer, taking a picture of a Frenchman can have some pretty serious consequences nowadays.

WALTER: You bet, Mr. Blank.

BLANK: No, no, that's against the law too. Accompanied by only three dozen officers, he started down the path to the shack. But this path was by no means easy. No, it was guarded by two mean Griddley Bears who lunged horribly right toward them. The party walked around them — then walked around them again.

WALTER: Was she finally taken in custody?

BLANK: Yes, the officers entered the one-room shack. Even then it took two days to reach the other side. Yes, the "one-room" shack was also a Zeppelin holder, or hanger, so-called because you could either hang the Zeppelin up when you weren't using it, or hold on to it. The Special Agent talked to the woman, stroking her gently, describing the pleasure of a seventy-five mile ride in a fast car. Well, she went willingly and later confidentially advised her Agent she liked the jail very much since she was steam-heated and had to be around a lot of water.

WALTER: You must be thinking of comely Lucy Bomeler, the 39-inch secretary to Kurt Klauspfeffer, the Nazi spy.

BLANK: I don't think I'll ever by able to stop thinking about her.

WALTER: Mr. Blank, I want to thank you for being here. You have given us all a new slant on the topic of Oriental Girls in crime and it has been most interesting. With you G-Men on the job we must feel sure that Nazi communes will surely be unsuccessful in their attempts, however vague, to injure our Area.

"TAPE" OVER, WE RETURN TO THE CORRESPONDENTS.

ERIC: Well, that doesn't seem to have much to do with the Presidential security arrangements . . .

WALTER (PP): That's — uh — true. I think that was the wrong

	tape — actually, I don't remember doing that interview . . .
ERIC:	Interesting stories, though. From a real old-timer. Reminds me of the Hoover Canary Sparrow Case of not so many years ago . . .
WALTER:	I'm sorry, Eric, but I understand that Charles is ready from Monster Island with a commentary on the day's events.

CHARLES IS DOING A STAND-UP.

CHARLES (PB):	The philosopher Pluto once said that if you look at the shadows on the Great Wall long enough, you'll see a Monster. Those words have a special absurdity here today — one that cannot be easily shaken off. Even for a man as shook up as the President. At first, things seemed suspiciously uneventful as the President's Roto-Bubble touched down at Edmund-Edmund Air Force Base on Monster Island. After the traditional 21-cheese bomb salute and ceremonial attack on the President's party, it was time, for the first time in a long time, to shake hands with some old enemies. Many will remember these two oldsters — King Kong and the once Mighty Joe Young. See how relaxed the President seems with his own contemporaries . . . Godzilla, Destroyer of New York, Rubbergon, Destroyer of Washington, TrueMan, Destroyer of Hiroshima. The President, Mz. President, and Adolph, exchange pleasantries with the three-headed King Gidera himself, Destroyer of Toyko. But the real surprise came at the end of the line — here — when the President was introduced to the one Monster he had not expected to meet. Yes, it was the ancient 17-foot Glutamoto, who, ages ago, vowed never to look upon a human face again. Masking his temporary terror, his hands fluttering nervously at his mask, the President nevertheless strides forward to embrace the knee of his venerable foe. Well — and here you can see it clearly — before the President can reach him, Glutamoto does the unexpected one

more time! That's a twenty-foot banner unfurling, barely missing the President's Atomic Secretary. The words, our Monstrologists tell us, mean exactly what they say — Stop Killing Lizards! A frightening disappointment to a man already terrified of living on this planet. And a big, mean shadow, stretches from Pluto's cave to the tall tail of the President's rocket. This is Charles B. Smith, at the bar of the Free Launch Room on Monster Island.

A QUICK CUT-AWAY TO A COMMERCIAL.

THE RAVEN (PP): Caw caw caw!

POE (PA): Hi, neighbors! I'm Edgar Allen Poe, Manager of Bird of Prey Motors, where you can follow the feathers to under the sign of the Black Bird.

THE RAVEN: If you've been turned down before — Nevermore! Caw! Caw!

POE: Yes, that's right, Nick! Even if you've been killed in an auto accident and can't get your driver's license back from the police, we'll help ya'l! You know, it usually takes a lawyer to help a doctor to cure a policeman. But if it's action you want, we're all actors here . . .

PETE: And here!

DAVE: And here!

POE: At all the Bird of Prey Garages in Gotham and Metropolis . . .

PETE: And now in Duckberg, dockside, at the corner of Sump and Pumpit Avenue!

POE: For precision auto salvage, body belts and transmission problems too, come to where the President stands behind every car — Birds of Prey Garages, serving the Tri-City Area since 10 o'clock . . .

THE RAVEN:	Every morning!
POE:	When do we close?
THE RAVEN:	Nevermore! Nevermore!
POE (WITH SINGERS):	I will stand upon my head Until this Bird is dead At the Bird of Prey, The Bird of Prey Garage!
DAVE:	Get a lube job with Edgar Allen Poe!

THE COMMERCIAL ENDS AND THE PARTY SEGUES TO A MUSIC BREAK — DOLLY PARTON'S VERSION OF "MULE SKINNER BLUES."

THE PARTY RETURNS FROM THE BAR SINISTER OF THE FOUR HOT GUYS ADULT MOTOR LODGE ON MONSTER ISLAND. CHARLES B. SMITH HAS AN IMPROVISED CONVERSATION WITH SOME GUYS AT THE BAR BEFORE A SONG FROM NICK DANGER AND THE ASPHALT ARABS AT THE PIANO BAR.

LOONS
Words and Music by Phil Austin

My friends are all crazy, they're mad as Loons
They talk all at once, it's a hundred tunes
You hear them at night as you push down the highway
It's Loons landing at some exclusive Loon flyway

CHORUS: And oh, oh, oh — can it be true
That there's no rest for the wicked
And no peace for us two

Now the laughers and screamers their crosstalk is incredible
It's all you can do to believe they're inedible
And policemen and doctors hover 'round the edges
As they drag in new converts and make them sign pledges

CHORUS: And oh, oh, oh — can it be true
That there's no rest for the wicked
And no peace for us two

Now me an' my sweetheart have tried to escape
We've secretly put down our thoughts on this tape
And we're sending it out to all who might hear
Don't you talk all at once or you'll wake up right here

CHORUS: And oh, oh, oh — can it be true
That there's no rest for the wicked
And no peace for us two

	A passage of Loons to their home in the sky
Don't tempt me a bit, I think I'll pass it right by
So listen up friends, now you've heard my sad tune
Don't be tempted to talk all at once, like a Loon
CHORUS:	And oh, oh, oh — can it be true
That there's no rest for the wicked
And no peace for us two

THE SONG FINISHED AND THE PROGRAM CUTS TO A COMMERCIAL.

PA:	Hello, friends, I'm Gary Firesign for Mr. Romano of Hollywood.
PP:	Yes, our triple year-end sale is going on now or my name isn't Wilson.
DO:	Or mine.
PB:	Or mine.
DO:	You see, I don't think you can run a business like ours without satisfaction to the customer.
PB:	People say to me, Eddie, the sincerest form of flattery I guess you'd call it is imitation.
PP:	Too bad, Steve. But that's just our little joke.
PA:	The dog isn't for sale. Not since Ralph was arrested have I been able to offer you a Demon at this sensational price. The Pres . . .
PP:	. . . ident said move those Demons and golly I just can't afford not to.
DO:	And you don't have to dress up at Mr. Ed's for Threads. There's no suit over 30 dollars . . .
PB:	Now that a major clothing manufacturer has closed its doors on . . .

PA:	A substance *known* as adenodene phosphate, crucial to hair growth.
PP:	And I wouldn't let my wife drive one of them after what the Pres . . .
PA:	. . . ident said about Ralph. I'm sitting down on the dog now because I wouldn't want to spoil your movie. Some call it a commercial, but I like to call it thanks for the interruption and what . . .
PP:	. . . ever kids — spills — or the dog *does* to the hood of your auto he's not . . .
PA:	. . . for sale. That's just our little joke.
PB:	I'd like to show you some pictures of men and women like yourself, in this area, men and women, *like yourselves* in various poses, sitting . . .
DO:	. . . on the cars, late at night when even Fletcher is gone. Yes, Fletcher must sleep sometime.
PA:	I couldn't stand on my head to give you a better deal so I think I'll just sit down here to rest my back. There are so many of these . . .
PB:	. . . Demons here now for me to be entirely comfortable.
PA:	And the puppy, well, I like to call him your friend and mine, my dog Sturm, and he . . .
PP:	. . . 's not for sale. Everything else certainly is . . .
PA:	Since the President arrested Ralph.
DO:	There are more Demons on the lot than a week ago, they're piling up. We can't . . .
PB:	. . . get rid of them and there's no one to talk to . . .

PA:	Not even this little fella here. I like to call him your friend and my friend . . .
DO:	My dog Sturm the Second . . .
PP:	He's not for sale. Like people in this area — men and women . . .
PB:	*Like yourselves . . .*
DO:	Who thump and run when the President says Sell Those Demons . . .
PA:	So I'll just sit over here and wait for them to come and get me and this fella here, who I like to call — stuffed. He's not . . .
PP:	For sale . . .
PB:	But millions are, just like him . . .
DO:	Men and women . . .
PB:	Like yourselves . . .
PP:	Who are making a fortune today . . .
PA:	Selling stuffed dogs as the streets . . .
PB:	Become full of Demons . . .
DO:	And no fit place for this little fella here.
PA:	I'd like . . .
PP:	To call him Sturm . . .
DO:	Und Drang . . .
PA:	But they won't let me. Now thanks for the interruption . . .
PB:	And back to your game.

THE FIRST HALF OF THE MARTIAN SPACE PARTY ENDED HERE WITH A MUSIC BREAK — HARRY NILSON'S "JUMP INTO THE FIRE."

THE PERFORMANCE CONTINUED WITH ACT ONE, SCENE ONE OF SHAKESPEARE'S "ANYTHYNGE YOU WANT TO." THE SCENE — ABOARD A SHIP AT SEA IN HEAVY WEATHER. SOUNDS OF WIND, CREAKING, WAVES, GULLS AND SHIP'S BELLS. TWO COURTIERS ENTER.

STORMENDRANG (PP): Hi ho, good Signor Happenstance! What drives thee up on deck?

HAPPENSTANCE (PB): My stomach's gone off course again, I fear.

STORM: What? Liked thee not the twice-empressed duck?

HAPPEN: Impressed indeed! That duck was never meant to be a sailor —

STORM: But now she sails! Look out below! Come, come! Come back below, O bilious Happenstance. O hallow'd Happenstance. Now hollow Happenstance.

EDMUND EDMUND (PA): (FROM OFF) Haloo! Haloo! What haps above?

STORM: See how our sweet Lord, young Edmund Edmund is beside himself with spleen. You've spoiled his holy victory o'er the homeless Parmisans by thy retreat.

HAPPEN: Full twenty times I've heard him pick that fight — and win!

ED ED (OFF): Ho! Hapless Happenstance! My dogged Stormendrain!

STORM: Hear him rant! I fear our host, the Chinese Captain, cannot understand a word he says.

HAPPEN: Luckier than we! I would this mission done and we were docked on Flegmland's wealthy banks and I at home in bed.

STORM:	You'll sleep in bed when Edmund Edmund, our explosive charge, is safe delivered to the Bishop's churchy seat.
HAPPEN:	When double Edmund rests in Castle Phlegm, they'll no one sleep!
TOP MAST SAILOR:	Storm ho!
PORT SAILOR:	A tempest breaks across the lee!
STARBOARD SAILOR:	Lightning starboard boils the sea!
STORM:	Look you, at the darkening of the light!
HAPPEN:	The Moon seems drowned in rain.
CAPT. JING:	(OFF) All hands on deck!
SAILOR:	Tie down the ropes!
ANOTHER SAILOR:	Pull, boys, pull! We'll not be Neptune's guests tonight!
CAPT. JING:	(ENTERING) Decrease sails! No starch in sheets!
SAILOR:	Aye, aye, Captain.
CAPT. JING:	And roll out the barrels!
STORM:	Those are my barrels! My servants are in those barrels!

STORMENDRANG EXITS AS EDMUND EDMUND ENTERS.

ED ED:	Znuts! What's happened to our righteous speed? Hath courage run aground? Must warlike virtue quail before the crowing gale? Whose order leaves us beached like mermaids on the rocks?
HAPPEN:	Twice noble friend, I fear a storm is blowing up our aft!

ED ED:	O fortunate Happenstance! This wind can blow us naught but good. Fold not the mast! Put on more sail!
CAPT. JING:	Much ado about nothing. Happen every twelfth night. Go way!
ED ED:	Go away? Where? Where do we go, but home to Phlegm. My Nuncle Bishop prays and pays for my return. Sit out this storm? Nay! A great white sail is what we need to clear the decks for what's in store to be our lot.
CAPT. JING:	As you like it. Anythynge you want to. Or, what you will.
ED ED:	Now, crack cheeks and break wind, break! We'll die at sea or live on land — for History's sake.

THE MOVIE, FOR SO IT IS, COMES TO A BREAK ON MONSTER ISLAND TV.

ROCKY (PB):	Well, that's pretty confusing so far. But if you think you're confusing now, you ain't seen nothing yet. And you may not, unless you stick around for the rest of this afternoon's Rocky Rocomoto Million Dollar Monster Classic — Anythynge You Want To by Shake-a-speare. Here on Your T-V — Monster Island, Channel Three. So watch this commercial message and then come back because later you can risk everything with our big contest, when we may call *you* to play "Now You See It, Now You Don't!" So watch carefully . . .

UNDERSCORE OF "JAPANESE" FLUTE MUSIC.

FLED MAY (PA):	Yes! All people come to Hideo Gump Senior's Rendevous Rump Room!
MS MAY (PP):	At top of Japanese-American Friendship Tower on Monster Island!

FLED:	Where the Boss is a man rike yourself. Hang out. Fright Night come right after Happi Hour every night. No Buddhists!
MS MAY:	At Hideo Gump Senior's Rend-rease Roast Room. It's Real Gong!

A REAL GONG.

HIDEO (DO):	Herro! Yes, this speaking sounds like Hideo Gump, Sr., and is! Yes, herro! This proud father speaking of son Hideo Gump. Couldn't be happier. Well-deserved success. But what is poor old dad to do? Can's "go on road" or "smoke weed." Suffering dilemma. So Hideo buy me restaurant. Come eat here. You might see him.
FLED:	So make it a habit! For powerful dining experience! Hideo Gump Senior's Rathskeller Rump Room!
MS MAY:	For a stable currency or a table by the fire . . .

THE TV PROGRAM RETURNS WITH THE NEXT PART OF "ANYTHYNGE." IT IS EARLY MORNING ON THE BATTLEMENTS OF CASTLE FLEGM. A COCK CROWS. PETE, A GUARD, WALKS BACK AND FORTH ON DUTY, SINGING.

PETE:	Oh, the Soldier's life it ain't so grand! Bend, boys, bend! But me feets at least are on dry land! Bend, boys, bend! Yare! I'll drink me sack 'til I'm on me back, While the Earth supports me fall. While the Sailor lad, when he's drunk and mad, Will sink like a tinker's ball! Oh, the Soldier's life it ain't so grand! Bend, boys, bend! But me feets . . .

THE SHEET-COVERED GHOST OF THE KING ENTERS.

GHOST:	Ooooooooooooo!

PETE:	'Od's balls! Tis the ghost! Evacuate into the morning mists, O dreadful wraith!
GHOST:	Oooooooooooooo!
PETE:	C-come not c-closer, s-spirit c-cold, or I'll shred yer sheets with the lance'lot bold!

THROWING OFF THE SHEET, ANOTHER GUARD REVEALS HIMSELF.

ANDREW:	Ha ha! Put up or pike, Pete! 'Tis I, Andrew Lunch, yer battle-mate.
PETE:	Me bottle-mate, you mean! Yer jest has put me pants afloat. It's only right for you to fill them up again.
ANDREW:	You quake and clank and drip with terror! A sorry mess! If fabled King Bernardo really walked, you'd turn to jelly!
PETE:	If I be jelly, where be me breakfast toast?
ANDREW:	Here's toast enough for both of us. Come, fill your cup.
PETE:	We'll meet the dawn with elbows up!
BOTH:	Bend, boys, bend!
GHOSTLY VOICE:	Oooooooooooooo!
ANDREW:	Who go'st there?
PETE:	A ghost, there upon the battlements.
ANDREW:	It seems to float with no more substance than me steamy breath!
PETE:	List! It speaks!
GHOST:	Now sleep sits moistly 'pon my face these clammy nights! Long oft I've walked upon these hoary,

	withering heights in aimless, mindless searching for a man with blunted aim and mobled tights.
ANDREW:	Mobled tights? That's good!
PETE:	Motley tights, he means. With spots.
ANDREW:	Spotted pants? There's but one man that fits in that conscription!
PETE:	And but one butt in spotted pants!
GHOST:	Edmu-u-u-u-u-nd!!
PETE:	Edmund?
ANDREW:	Edmund!
GHOST:	Not Edmund Edmund, but rightful Edmund, happy Edmund, princely Edmund!
ANDREW:	He means drunken Edmund! I know the nook in which he sleeps the night away. I'll get him flat!

ANDREW LEAVES AND THE GHOST ADVANCES.

GHOST:	I grow cold! I grow cold! Night slips away!
PETE:	As does thy slip! Uncovering blue and goosy flesh!
GHOST:	Ghostly flesh, rather. Nay! Touch me not!

ANDREW RE-ENTERS WITH EDMUND.

ED:	Where is it? Show it to me!
ANDREW:	It climbs toward King Bernardo's crumbling tower, my lord.
ED:	Hand me my sword-flask, varlet!
ANDREW:	What use your steel against a ghost?

ED: Methought you spoke of *goats* upon the battlements!

ANDREW: Nay, ghost, my lord.

ED: Be he goat or ghost or boat or both, I'll spirits need to goad my spirits on.

PETE: Take speed, my lord! The spook would speak with thee! See where he hops up to the tower's top!

GHOST: Edmu-u-u-u-und!

ED: He's flushed me out! As was writ in antique script! This doth portend deep trenchery and muddy secrets to be told.

PETE: He beckons!

ANDREW: And he stamps his naked feet upon the slippery stone.

ED: Go not, inpatient spirit, for now I come!

ANDREW: Take care, Master, that he lead thee not to Hell!

ED: Not to Hell? What Hell? What's Hell to me or me to Hell? As a tot 'twas told me not to cross the moat, but then the Monk he did bespeak me castle moat from mine own eye! So thus I crossed my eyes and double-crossed the Monk, who fell into the moat, the dolt! Then soon they bade me warning that I play not by myself — 'twill make me blind! But I was deaf and so I jumped into the burning bush and lo! Altho' consumed, I rose again to bite another apple on yet another Eve! I spit out half a snake! Afraid of Hell? I've left my senses many times and drempt I fought great monsters — pink Behemoths, rats upon my bed! Who cares? I've been in service of the Marshall Mars and viewed blue skies turned rusty by the reddened dust — seen good green Earth all yellow-soaked with fear — blood-covered, blistered, black-pocked like

Luna's back! Foo! Are we not men? If we fall, can we not rise again? Hot-headed, flushed with blood, we'll take it lying down, we'll take it standing up, we'll get it anyway we can! Take this! Saint Mickey, save me! I'll wiggle my ears and march forth full of song and give my finger to the first who follows not! See? There he stands!

GHOST: Shut up, Edmund!

EDMUND ADVANCES WITH HIS SWORD, THE GHOST GRABS HIM AND THEN CHASES HIM OFF.

ED: You get my point? Let go! Let go! Let's go! Have-at-choo!

PETE: Gazundheit! Poor Master . . .

ANDREW: Brave fool!

PETE: Barefoot, say you? Brave fool, say you? After all, he is a Prince, the Minstrels sing.

ANDREW: Among men, yes. Among fools, he is a King!

AS THE GUARDS MARCH OFF, THE PROGRAM ENDS AND RETURNS TO THE HOST.

ROCKY: . . . 'econd part of this Classic Feature will come to you tomorrow afternoon, if you can take it. Now, my favorite part of Rocky Rocomoto's Million Dollar Monster Classic — the adventures of our great local Oriental hero — Young Guy, Safety Rider!!

STRANGE "JAPANESE" MUSIC ON FLUTE AND WOODBLOCK THROUGHOUT.

ANNOUNCER: (SOTO VOCE) We left last week where we found it after fortunate encounter with Radio Prison. Now out, Young Guy holds on to Miki for exposition . . .

MIKI: Oh, Young Guy! Oh gosh! You back! Worried feeling!

GUY: Now, baby, don't be crying. Now I'm out and wishing I had a drink. Where is Rotonoto?

ROTONOTO: Here, Boss! It Hurry Gurry Hour. Have Special Motor Fluid Gimlet. Say, what happened to Prison at today?

GUY: Lt. Brad Shaw of Motorfficial Cops sniffing up our little secret, I think.

MIKI: O Young Guy — like little tears my terrific feelings for it — like little flowers.

GUY: Yes.

ROTO: What is it we are about to be doing, Boss? Are we taking motorcycles? Are we taking Atom Bus? Are we stepping in speedy Cruiser Boat? Do we have time to take a fast train?

GUY: Don't be torturing me! You see, in Radio Prison they washed the brain of this unfortunate, hanging up on a strong seagull-wind, now to dry; but the maiden upon taking it into her warm kitchen finds the owner not there!

MIKI: Pretty words, but come to conclusion, beloved!

GUY: Terrible! Decision-making factor absent from brain.

MIKI: No. Imprecations many, all terrible! Which Motor are we about to be riding in?

GUY: Not to be torturing me!

ROTO: Boss! Boss! New character enter! Announcing Lt. Brad Shaw, Atomic Occupation Forces.

MIKI: O Young Guy! Now we only take familiar ride to Radio Prison!

BRAD SHAW BUSTS IN.

BRAD: O. K. Guy! This is putting every little piece of the puzzle in now! It was you, Young Guy, who is snooping in Official Business? Did the trick of Radio Prison — is it funny now? Do you see?

OTHER THREE: What?

BRAD: Now I know where the Dream Monsters come. What is Glutamoto the Horror of Toyko beside total fiendish quality of you brain. They all you! Glutamoto dumn everything. This is not bad enough? Yes! There is also Gorgonzola the Cheese Monster.

GUY: Being easy, man. Let's be keeping cool. How am I to be Atom Monsters, Lt. Brad Shaw when . . . Just keeping still one moment. Your name "Brad Shaw." What "Brad" standing up for?

BRAD: Bernard.

GUY:	Gosh! You George Bernard Shaw — famous author and smart guy.
MIKI:	Oh, Young Guy! You figure it all out!
ROTO:	I see, Boss! Brad Shaw say many times he on side of right.
BRAD:	That's right . . .
ROTO:	That because he *writer*!
GUY:	In obvious pun lies subtle secret, Rotonoto. Writer responsible for all problems he create.
BRAD:	Wait a minute! Hold it! You not going to pinning this Monster rap on me.

HE SOCKS YOUNG GUY AND A TREMENDOUS FIGHT FOLLOWS IN WHICH BOTH BRAD SHAW AND YOUNG GUY ARE KNOCKED OUT.

MIKI:	Oh, Rotonoto! You knock them both out with champain gong.
ROTO:	I wait long time for this. No more nice guy. You go with me now, baby. I got two tickets for Forbidden City!
MIKI:	Oh! Even President not get in there!
ROTO:	And next week this show have new name! "Rotonoto, Atomic Gumshoe." And no Buddhist writer, either. Common, baby! We got road to travel!
MIKI:	Oh, Roto! You some Atomic Guy!

A FLOURISH OF FLUTE BRINGS THE EPISODE TO A CLOSE. THE PROGRAM TAKES A MUSIC BREAK WITH "INSIDE LOOKING OUT" BY THE SPIDERS.

WHEN THE MARTIAN SPACE PARTY RETURNS, WE ARE IN THE SPACE BUBBLE, SOMEWHERE IN ORBIT. THE FIREBELLES ARE HUMMING BEHIND THE ANNOUNCER, BEFORE THEY BURST INTO SONG.

ANNOUNCER: Hello, hello! Yes, that sentimental old refrain, "Lorraine, Lorraine" brings memories back to the old Space Bubble brain. You're a member of the Spacepipe Club — you've got the key — so unsnap your spacesuit and close the airlock behind you, 'cause you're in Hilerio Spacepipe's free-fallin' pad — and, shhhhh! He's listening, while the cool Firebelles turn in the alarm . . .

FIREBELLES:
Lorraine, Lorraine,
You're on the wrong train.
Lorraine, Lorraine,
You're in the wrong lane.
Lorraine, Lorraine,
It's driving me insane.
Lorraine, Lorraine,
The rain, the rain.
Insane though I may be
I think I've found another one like me.

THE AUDIENCE APPLAUDS AND HILERIO MAKES HIS ENTRANCE.

HILERIO: Ahoy, maties! This is old Hilerio Spacepipe here, pilot of my own bedroom, past-master of my own density. Well, we've just planted the Good Time Flag on the sandbars of Saturn. The smoking lamp is most definitely lit . . .

TWIXIE: It looks like an old Pirate Ship movie, Hilerio. And you — you look like Errol Flynn in a spacesuit!

HILERIO: And you, Twixie — you look like Rhonda Flemming. Help, help me Rhonda! Glove on that! What a co-pilot, what a gal! Twixie Slowblow, Queen of the Space Rats!

TWIXIE: It's my year!

HILERIO: Backing us up against the Bubble wall, making the music of the spheres, your favorites and I hope they're mine — Nick Danger and the Asphalt Arabs! He's not so good at talking while he's playing, so

GUY:	Gosh! You George Bernard Shaw — famous author and smart guy.
MIKI:	Oh, Young Guy! You figure it all out!
ROTO:	I see, Boss! Brad Shaw say many times he on side of right.
BRAD:	That's right . . .
ROTO:	That because he *writer*!
GUY:	In obvious pun lies subtle secret, Rotonoto. Writer responsible for all problems he create.
BRAD:	Wait a minute! Hold it! You not going to pinning this Monster rap on me.

HE SOCKS YOUNG GUY AND A TREMENDOUS FIGHT FOLLOWS IN WHICH BOTH BRAD SHAW AND YOUNG GUY ARE KNOCKED OUT.

MIKI:	Oh, Rotonoto! You knock them both out with champain gong.
ROTO:	I wait long time for this. No more nice guy. You go with me now, baby. I got two tickets for Forbidden City!
MIKI:	Oh! Even President not get in there!
ROTO:	And next week this show have new name! "Rotonoto, Atomic Gumshoe." And no Buddhist writer, either. Common, baby! We got road to travel!
MIKI:	Oh, Roto! You some Atomic Guy!

A FLOURISH OF FLUTE BRINGS THE EPISODE TO A CLOSE. THE PROGRAM TAKES A MUSIC BREAK WITH "INSIDE LOOKING OUT" BY THE SPIDERS.

WHEN THE MARTIAN SPACE PARTY RETURNS, WE ARE IN THE SPACE BUBBLE, SOMEWHERE IN ORBIT. THE FIREBELLES ARE HUMMING BEHIND THE ANNOUNCER, BEFORE THEY BURST INTO SONG.

ANNOUNCER: Hello, hello! Yes, that sentimental old refrain, "Lorraine, Lorraine" brings memories back to the old Space Bubble brain. You're a member of the Spacepipe Club — you've got the key — so unsnap your spacesuit and close the airlock behind you, 'cause you're in Hilerio Spacepipe's free-fallin' pad — and, shhhhh! He's listening, while the cool Firebelles turn in the alarm . . .

FIREBELLES: Lorraine, Lorraine,
You're on the wrong train.
Lorraine, Lorraine,
You're in the wrong lane.
Lorraine, Lorraine,
It's driving me insane.
Lorraine, Lorraine,
The rain, the rain.
Insane though I may be
I think I've found another one like me.

THE AUDIENCE APPLAUDS AND HILERIO MAKES HIS ENTRANCE.

HILERIO: Ahoy, maties! This is old Hilerio Spacepipe here, pilot of my own bedroom, past-master of my own density. Well, we've just planted the Good Time Flag on the sandbars of Saturn. The smoking lamp is most definitely lit . . .

TWIXIE: It looks like an old Pirate Ship movie, Hilerio. And you — you look like Errol Flynn in a spacesuit!

HILERIO: And you, Twixie — you look like Rhonda Flemming. Help, help me Rhonda! Glove on that! What a co-pilot, what a gal! Twixie Slowblow, Queen of the Space Rats!

TWIXIE: It's my year!

HILERIO: Backing us up against the Bubble wall, making the music of the spheres, your favorites and I hope they're mine — Nick Danger and the Asphalt Arabs! He's not so good at talking while he's playing, so

GUY:	Gosh! You George Bernard Shaw — famous author and smart guy.
MIKI:	Oh, Young Guy! You figure it all out!
ROTO:	I see, Boss! Brad Shaw say many times he on side of right.
BRAD:	That's right . . .
ROTO:	That because he *writer*!
GUY:	In obvious pun lies subtle secret, Rotonoto. Writer responsible for all problems he create.
BRAD:	Wait a minute! Hold it! You not going to pinning this Monster rap on me.

HE SOCKS YOUNG GUY AND A TREMENDOUS FIGHT FOLLOWS IN WHICH BOTH BRAD SHAW AND YOUNG GUY ARE KNOCKED OUT.

MIKI:	Oh, Rotonoto! You knock them both out with champain gong.
ROTO:	I wait long time for this. No more nice guy. You go with me now, baby. I got two tickets for Forbidden City!
MIKI:	Oh! Even President not get in there!
ROTO:	And next week this show have new name! "Rotonoto, Atomic Gumshoe." And no Buddhist writer, either. Common, baby! We got road to travel!
MIKI:	Oh, Roto! You some Atomic Guy!

A FLOURISH OF FLUTE BRINGS THE EPISODE TO A CLOSE. THE PROGRAM TAKES A MUSIC BREAK WITH "INSIDE LOOKING OUT" BY THE SPIDERS.

WHEN THE MARTIAN SPACE PARTY RETURNS, WE ARE IN THE SPACE BUBBLE, SOMEWHERE IN ORBIT. THE FIREBELLES ARE HUMMING BEHIND THE ANNOUNCER, BEFORE THEY BURST INTO SONG.

ANNOUNCER: Hello, hello! Yes, that sentimental old refrain, "Lorraine, Lorraine" brings memories back to the old Space Bubble brain. You're a member of the Spacepipe Club — you've got the key — so unsnap your spacesuit and close the airlock behind you, 'cause you're in Hilerio Spacepipe's free-fallin' pad — and, shhhhh! He's listening, while the cool Firebelles turn in the alarm . . .

FIREBELLES: Lorraine, Lorraine,
You're on the wrong train.
Lorraine, Lorraine,
You're in the wrong lane.
Lorraine, Lorraine,
It's driving me insane.
Lorraine, Lorraine,
The rain, the rain.
Insane though I may be
I think I've found another one like me.

THE AUDIENCE APPLAUDS AND HILERIO MAKES HIS ENTRANCE.

HILERIO: Ahoy, maties! This is old Hilerio Spacepipe here, pilot of my own bedroom, past-master of my own density. Well, we've just planted the Good Time Flag on the sandbars of Saturn. The smoking lamp is most definitely lit . . .

TWIXIE: It looks like an old Pirate Ship movie, Hilerio. And you — you look like Errol Flynn in a spacesuit!

HILERIO: And you, Twixie — you look like Rhonda Flemming. Help, help me Rhonda! Glove on that! What a co-pilot, what a gal! Twixie Slowblow, Queen of the Space Rats!

TWIXIE: It's my year!

HILERIO: Backing us up against the Bubble wall, making the music of the spheres, your favorites and I hope they're mine — Nick Danger and the Asphalt Arabs! He's not so good at talking while he's playing, so